SUMMER MATH WORKBOOK

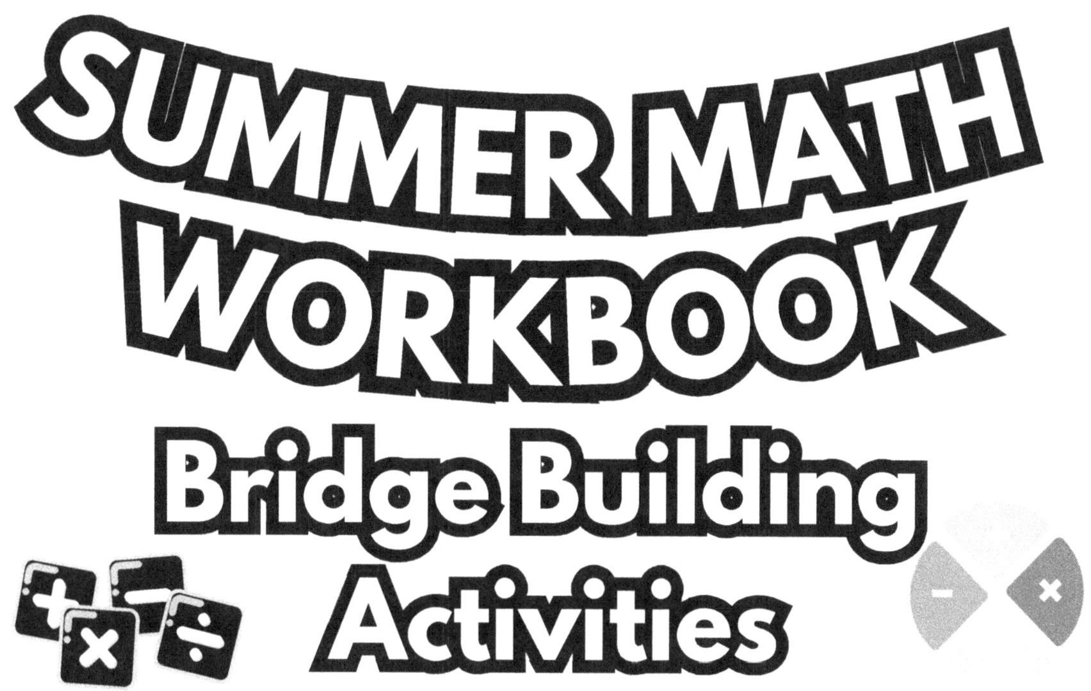

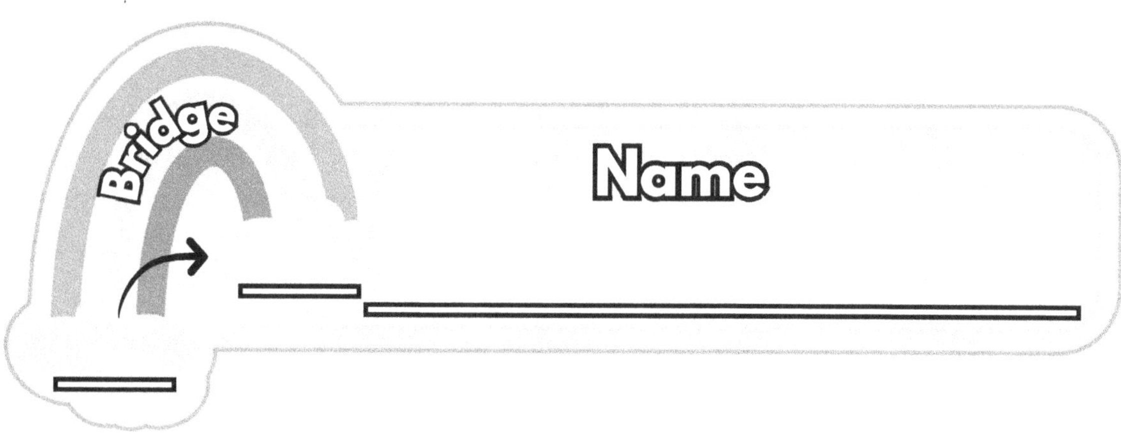

Introduction

As parents and educators, we understand the pivotal role that mathematics plays in shaping a child's academic journey and future success. Yet, the path to mathematical proficiency can often seem daunting, filled with challenges and complexities. That's where the transformative power of Summer Bridge Building Activities books comes into play, illuminating the way forward with clarity, precision, and purpose.

Summer vacation is a time for rest and relaxation, but it also presents the risk of the "summer slide," where students lose some of the academic gains they made during the school year. Summer Bridge Building Activities books are specifically designed to tackle this challenge, ensuring that your child stays academically engaged and prepared for the upcoming school year. These books provide a seamless bridge from one grade to the next, reinforcing essential skills and introducing new concepts that will give your child a head start.

Imagine your child eagerly diving into the pages of a Summer Bridge Building Activities book, greeted by clear, engaging content that demystifies complex mathematical concepts. With each turn of the pages, they embark on a journey of discovery, encountering thoughtfully curated practice questions that reinforce learning and sharpen problem-solving skills. As they unveil the answers to those questions, a sense of accomplishment blossoms within them — a tangible reward for their hard work and dedication.

Summer Bridge Building Activities books transcend traditional educational tools; they are meticulously crafted to build a deep and enduring understanding of mathematics. These books follow a sequential and logical progression, starting from fundamental principles and advancing to sophisticated problem-solving strategies. Each chapter is designed to build on the previous one, ensuring a solid and comprehensive foundation for future learning.

Parents, we yearn for nothing more than to see our children thrive academically and personally. We want to witness the spark of inspiration ignited within them as they overcome academic challenges with confidence and poise. Summer Bridge Building Activities books serve as indispensable partners in this noble endeavor, offering not just practice questions but the keys to unlocking a world of academic and personal opportunities.

Visualize the pride on your child's face as they master a challenging math concept, the joy they experience when their efforts yield results, and the confidence they gain with each success. These pages are designed to make learning math a positive, enriching, and deeply rewarding experience that will benefit them throughout their academic journey and beyond.

For educators, Summer Bridge Building Activities books are invaluable allies in the quest to cultivate mathematical proficiency in the classroom. Accompanied by comprehensive guides and readily available answers, instructors can focus on mentoring and nurturing their students, secure in the knowledge that these books provide a robust framework for effective learning.

Within the pages of Summer Bridge Building Activities books lies not just the promise of academic excellence, but the seeds of a brighter future. By integrating these resources into your child's summer routine, you are bestowing upon them the gifts of confidence, curiosity, and a lifelong love of learning.

Invest in your child's future today with Summer Bridge Building Activities books — because every great journey begins with a single step, and this step can change everything. Keep the momentum of learning alive over the summer, and watch your child soar to new academic heights.

Contents

Grade
1 2
SUMMER MATH
WORKBOOK
Bridge Building
Activities
Number Sense
Addition and Subtraction
Place Value

Grade
2 3
SUMMER MATH
WORKBOOK
Bridge Building
Activities
Number Sense
Addition and Subtraction
Place Value

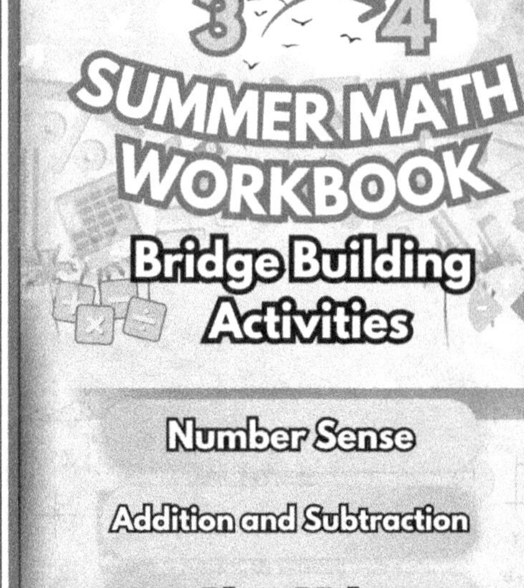

Grade
3 4
SUMMER MATH
WORKBOOK
Bridge Building
Activities
Number Sense
Addition and Subtraction
Place Value

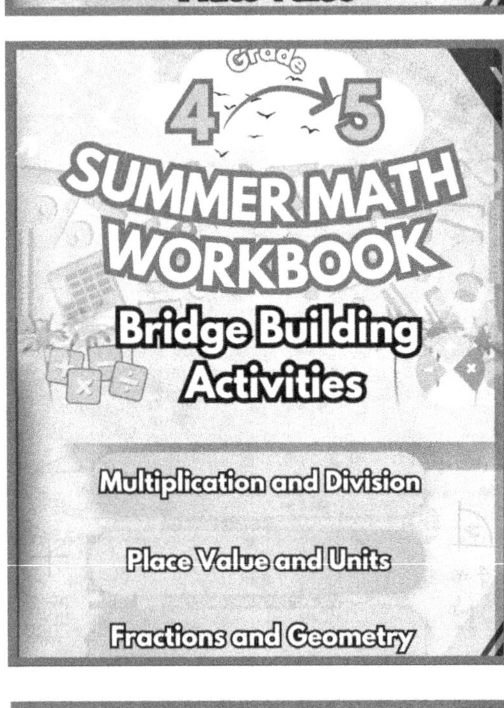

Grade
4 5
SUMMER MATH
WORKBOOK
Bridge Building
Activities
Multiplication and Division
Place Value and Units
Fractions and Geometry

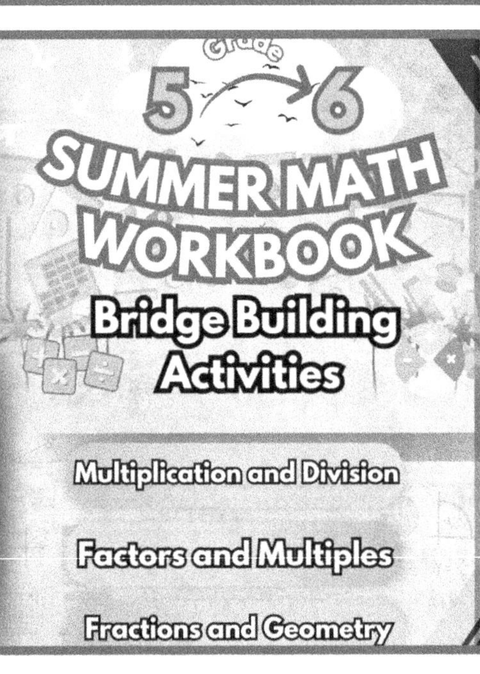

Grade
5 6
SUMMER MATH
WORKBOOK
Bridge Building
Activities
Multiplication and Division
Factors and Multiples
Fractions and Geometry

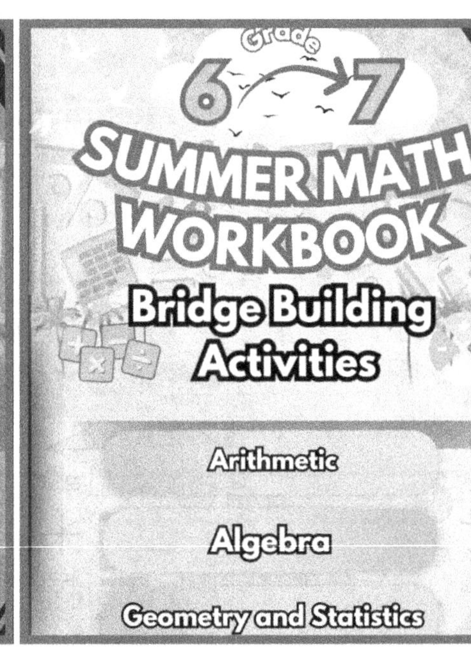

Grade
6 7
SUMMER MATH
WORKBOOK
Bridge Building
Activities
Arithmetic
Algebra
Geometry and Statistics

Grade
7 8
SUMMER MATH
WORKBOOK
Bridge Building
Activities
Ratio and Percentage
Algebra and Cartesian Plane
Geometry and Statistics

Grade
8 9
SUMMER MATH
WORKBOOK
Bridge Building
Activities
Ratio and Percentage
Algebra
Geometry and Graphing

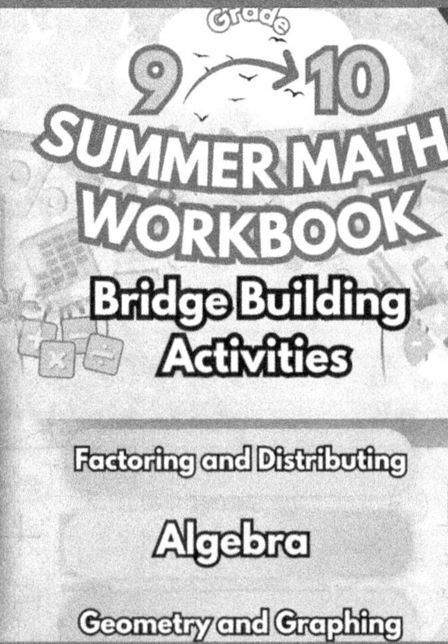

Grade
9 10
SUMMER MATH
WORKBOOK
Bridge Building
Activities
Factoring and Distributing
Algebra
Geometry and Graphing

<u>Multiplication and Division</u>

<u>Multiplication</u>

Multiplication is an easy way of adding numbers together quickly. Instead of adding the same number repeatedly, we use multiplication to find the total much faster.

> For instance, rather than adding 2 + 2 + 2 + 2 + 2, we can multiply 2 by 5 to get the same result: 2 x 5 = 10.

Here, the first number (2) is called the multiplicand, second number (5) is the multiplier. The answer we get, in this case, 10, is called the product.

> Let's think of multiplication as repeated addition.

> Take 2 x 5, for example. It means adding 2 together five times, which we can illustrate as: 2 + 2 + 2 + 2 + 2 = 10

Multiplication can also be visualized as groups of objects. Imagine we have 2 groups, each containing 5 oranges.

> To find the total number of oranges, we multiply the number of groups (2) by the number of oranges in each group (5):

> 2 groups of 5 oranges = 10 oranges

> Expressed as multiplication: 2 x 5 = 10

In summary, multiplication offers various ways to approach it: through repeated addition or by envisioning groups of objects. It's a powerful tool that makes solving math problems much quicker and more efficient!

<u>**Long Division and Remainders**</u>

Division is like the opposite of multiplication. It's all about sharing or distributing items equally among a certain number of groups or people.

When we divide one number by another, we're essentially splitting a number into equal parts. We're figuring out how many groups of a certain size can be made from that number.

For instance, let's divide 20 by 4.

When we divide 20 by 4, we're essentially asking, "How many groups of size 4 can we make from 20?"

Now, there are several parts or terms involved in the division process:

- **Dividend:** This is the number being divided, which in this case, is 20.

- **Divisor:** This is the number we're dividing by, which is 4.

- **Quotient:** This is the answer we get after dividing. It tells us how many groups of divisors can be made from the dividend. In this case, the answer is 5.

- **Remainder:** when the divisor doesn't evenly divide the dividend, we get the remainder.

So, when we divide 20 by 4, we found out that 5 groups of 4 can be made from 20.

Let's solve problems from exercises:

$$\begin{array}{r} 4 \\ 4\overline{)16} \\ -16 \\ \hline 0 \end{array}$$

$$\begin{array}{r} 42 \\ 12\overline{)504} \\ -48 \\ \hline 24 \\ -24 \\ \hline 0 \end{array}$$

$$\begin{array}{r} 477 \\ 6\overline{)2{,}862} \\ -24 \\ \hline 46 \\ -42 \\ \hline 42 \\ -42 \\ \hline 0 \end{array}$$

$$\begin{array}{r} 8{,}965 \text{ R1} \\ 9\overline{)80{,}686} \\ -72 \\ \hline 86 \\ -81 \\ \hline 58 \\ -54 \\ \hline 46 \\ -45 \\ \hline 1 \end{array}$$

Multiplying Decimals

Multiplying decimals is a lot like multiplying whole numbers, but we need to be careful about where we put the decimal point in the answer.

Step 1: Start by multiplying the numbers together, just like we do with whole numbers. Ignore the decimals for now.

Step 2: Count how many decimal places there are in the numbers we're multiplying. This will tell us how many decimal places our answer should have.

Step 3: Put the decimal point in the answer by starting from the right side of the number. Move the decimal point to the left as many places as there are in the total number of decimal places.

For example, let's multiply 4.5 by 2.5:

Step 1: Multiply the numbers as if they were whole numbers:

$$25 \times 45 = 1125.$$

Step 2: There is one decimal place in 2.5 and one in 4.5, making a total of two decimal places.

Step 3: Starting from the right side of the answer, count two places to the left and put the decimal point there.

So, the final answer is 11.25.

Remember to pay close attention to where the decimal point goes in the answer.

Dividing Decimals

Dividing decimals is a lot like dividing whole numbers, but we need to be careful about placement of decimal point in the answer.

Steps to follow:

1. **Set up the division problem:** Write the dividend (the number being divided) and the divisor (the number you're dividing by) as you would in a long division problem.

$$1.7 \overline{)1.6}$$

2. **Move the decimal:** Move the decimal point to the right in the dividend and divisor by the same number of places.

$$17 \overline{)16}$$

3. **Perform the division:** Divide as you would with whole numbers.

$$
\begin{array}{r}
0\,0.9\,4 \\
17\overline{)16} \\
-\,0 \\
\hline
1\,6 \\
-\,0 \\
\hline
1\,6\,0 \\
-1\,5\,3 \\
\hline
7\,0 \\
-6\,8 \\
\hline
2
\end{array}
$$

4. **Place the decimal point:** Place the decimal point in the quotient directly above its position in the dividend.

So, the quotient is 0.94.

Using the Power of 10

Using the powers of 10, 100, and 1000 makes multiplying and dividing by these numbers very convenient. Let's illustrate with examples:

Multiplying by Powers of 10:

- To multiply a number by 10, simply move the decimal point one place to the right.

$$5 \times 10 = 50$$

- To multiply a number by 100, move the decimal point two places to the right.

$$5 \times 100 = 500$$

- To multiply a number by 1000, move the decimal point three places to the right.

$$5 \times 1000 = 5000.$$

Dividing by Powers of 10:

- To divide a number by 10, simply move the decimal point one place to the left.

$$50 \div 10 = 5$$

- To divide a number by 100, move the decimal point two places to the left.

$$500 \div 100 = 5$$

- To divide a number by 1000, move the decimal point three places to the left.

$$5000 \div 1000 = 5$$

Using the powers of 10, 100, and 1000 makes multiplying and dividing by these numbers simple and straightforward.

<u>**Place Value and Expanded Notations**</u>

Place value tells us the value of a digit in a number based on where it's placed.

Consider the number **565,347.236**. It consists of nine digits: 5, 6, 5, 3, 4, 7, 2, 3, and 6.

Digit	Place Value Position	Value Calculation	Value
5	Hundred thousands place	5 × 100,000	500,000
6	Ten thousands place	6 × 10,000	60,000
5	Thousands place	5 × 1,000	5,000
3	Hundreds place	3 × 100	300
4	Tens place	4 × 10	40
7	Ones place	7 × 1	7
2	Tenths place	2 × 0.1	0.2
3	Hundredths place	3 × 0.01	0.03
6	Thousandths place	6 × 0.001	0.006

Each digit occupies a unique position:

- The digit **5** is in the hundred thousands place, signifying five groups of 100,000.

- The digit **6** is in the ten thousands place, indicating six groups of 10,000.

- The digit **5** is in the thousands place, representing five groups of 1,000.

- The digit **3** is in the hundreds place, representing three groups of 100.

- The digit **4** is in the tens place, representing four groups of 10.

- The digit **7** is in the ones place, representing seven single units.

- The digit **2** is in the tenths place, representing two groups of 0.1.

- The digit **3** is in the hundredths place, representing three groups of 0.01.

- The digit **6** is in the thousandths place, representing six groups of 0.001.

To find the total value of the number **565,347.236**, we calculate the value of each digit based on its place:

- The digit **5** in the hundred thousands place equals 500,000.

- The digit **6** in the ten thousands place equals 60,000.

- The digit **5** in the thousands place equals 5,000.

- The digit **3** in the hundreds place equals 300.

- The digit **4** in the tens place equals 40.

- The digit **7** in the ones place equals 7.

- The digit **2** in the tenths place equals 0.2.

- The digit **3** in the hundredths place equals 0.03.

- The digit **6** in the thousandths place equals 0.006.

By summing these values, we determine the overall value of the number:

500,000 + 60,000 + 5,000 + 300 + 40 + 7 + 0.2 + 0.03 + 0.006 = 565,347.236

Fractions

Fractions represent parts of a whole. They consist of a numerator (the number on top) and a denominator (the number on the bottom).

For example: we have an orange, and we divide it into 5 equal slices. Each slice represents $\frac{1}{5}$ of the orange. Now, if we take 3 of those slices, we have taken $\frac{3}{5}$ of the orange.

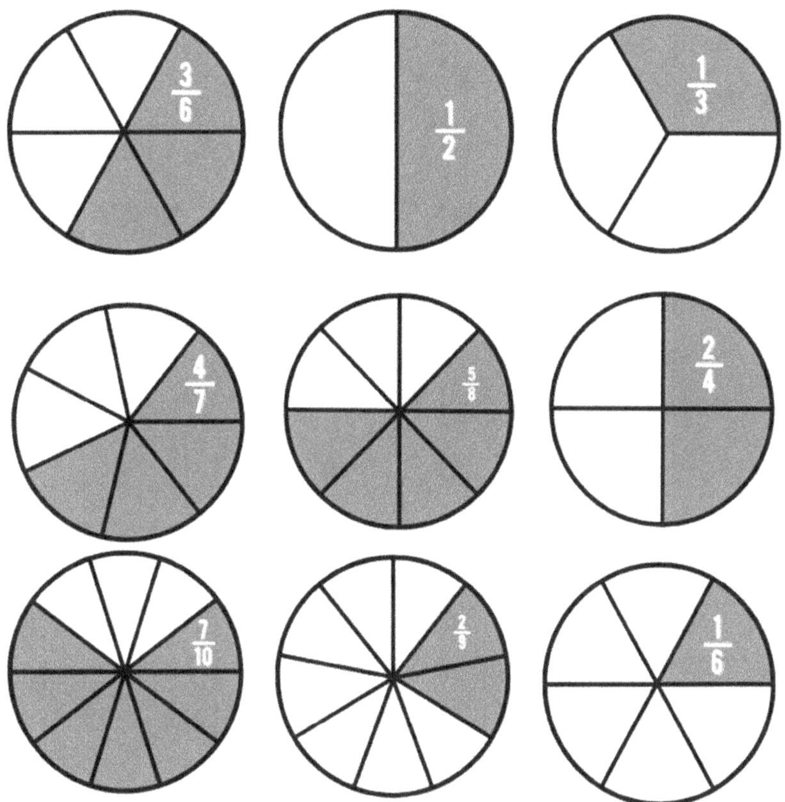

Equivalent Fractions

Equivalent fractions are fractions that represent the same value or part of a whole, even though they may look different.

To find equivalent fractions, you can:

- Multiply or divide both the numerator and denominator by the same nonzero number.
- Simplify fractions to their simplest form.

$\frac{1}{2}$ and $\frac{2}{4}$ are equivalent fractions because if you multiply the numerator and denominator of $\frac{1}{2}$ by 2, you get $\frac{2}{4}$. Similarly, if you divide both the numerator and denominator of $\frac{2}{4}$ by 2, you get $\frac{1}{2}$.

Let's solve a problem:

$$\frac{}{8} = \frac{15}{40}$$

To solve the missing numerator, we can cross multiply.

$$40x = 8 \times 15$$

$$40x = 120$$

$$x = \frac{120}{40} = x = 3$$

$$\frac{3}{8} = \frac{15}{40}$$

Least Common Multiple (LCM)

The Lowest Common Multiple (LCM) of two or more numbers is the smallest multiple that is divisible by each of the numbers.

There are several methods to find the LCM; however, we will focus on only two:

Listing Multiples: List the multiples of each number until you find a common multiple. For example:

$$\begin{array}{l|l} 8 & 8,\ 16,\ 24,\ 32,\ 40,\ 48,\ 56 \\ \hline 7 & 7,\ 14,\ 21,\ 28,\ 35,\ 42,\ 49,\ 56 \end{array} \quad , \ \text{LCM} = \underline{56}$$

Division Method: Divide each number with the smallest prime number that divides at least one of the numbers evenly. The product of all the divisors and quotients is the LCM. For example:

$$\begin{array}{c|cc} 2 & 7 & 8 \\ \hline 2 & 7 & 4 \\ \hline 2 & 7 & 2 \\ \hline 7 & 7 & 1 \\ \hline & 1 & 1 \end{array}$$

$$\text{LCM} = 2 \times 2 \times 2 \times 7 = \underline{56}$$

Both methods have their advantages. For big numbers, using the division way is usually faster. But if we are working with smaller numbers or like seeing patterns, listing multiples might make more sense.

Fractions Addition (Uncommon Denominator)

When adding fractions with uncommon denominators, we need to find a common denominator before we can add them. We will follow the following steps:

1. **Find the Least Common Denominator (LCD).** Determine the least common multiple (LCM) of the denominators.
2. **Convert fractions to have the common denominator :** Rewrite each fraction so that it has the common denominator found in step 1. To do

this, multiply the numerator and denominator of each fraction by the same value to make the denominators the same.

3. **Add the fractions:** Once the fractions have the same denominator, add the numerators together and keep the denominator the same.

4. **Simplify, if necessary:** If possible, simplify the resulting fraction by reducing it to its simplest form.

For example, let's add:

$$\frac{5}{11} + \frac{1}{4}$$

The LCM = 2 x 2 x 11 = <u>44</u>

$$\frac{5\times4 + 1\times11}{11\times4} = \frac{20 + 11}{44}$$

$$\frac{31}{44}$$

Fractions Subtraction (Uncommon Denominator)

Fractions subtraction with uncommon denominator follows the same steps except that we subtract instead of adding the fractions.

For example:

$$\frac{5}{11} - \frac{1}{4}$$

The LCM = 2 x 2 x 11 = <u>44</u>

$$\frac{5\times4 - 1\times11}{11\times4} = \frac{20 - 11}{44}$$

$$\frac{9}{44}$$

<u>**Fractions Multiplication**</u>

To multiply fractions, we simply multiply the numerators together to get the new numerator and multiply the denominators together to get the new denominator.

For example, let's multiply: $\frac{2}{4} \times \frac{1}{4}$

Numerator: $2 \times 1 = 2$

Denominator: $4 \times 4 = 16$

Therefore, $\frac{2}{16}$

we can simplify the resulting fraction: $\frac{1}{8}$

Let's solve a problem:

$$\frac{4}{5} \times \frac{4}{5} = \frac{4 \times 4}{5 \times 5} = \frac{16}{25}$$

<u>**Fractions Division**</u>

To divide fractions, we multiply by the reciprocal of the divisor.

For example, let's divide:

$$\frac{6}{8} \div \frac{4}{8}$$

$$\frac{6}{8} \times \frac{8}{4} = \frac{48}{32} = \frac{3}{2}$$

Geometry

Area and Perimeter

The area of a shape represents the amount of space it occupies. The perimeter of a shape is the total distance around its outer edge.

Area of Rectangle

For a square, since all four sides are equal, we only need to know the length of one side to find its area. We can calculate the area of a square by multiplying the length of one side by itself (squared). So, if the length of one side of the square is 's', then the area (A) is given by:

$A = s \times s$

4 in

4 in

$A = 4 \times 4$

$A = 16$

Perimeter of Rectangle

For a square, since all four sides are equal, we can find the perimeter by adding up the lengths of all four sides. If 's' represents the length of one side, then the perimeter (P) is given by:

$$P = 4 \times s$$

$$P = 4 \times 4$$

$$P = 16$$

Area of Triangle:

The area of a triangle represents the amount of space enclosed within its three sides. The formula for calculating the area of a triangle depends on the type of triangle. For a general triangle, we use the formula:

$$A = \frac{1}{2} \times \text{base} \times \text{height}$$

Where:

- *A* represents the area of the triangle.

- The base is the length of any one side of the triangle.

- The height is the perpendicular distance from the base to the opposite vertex.

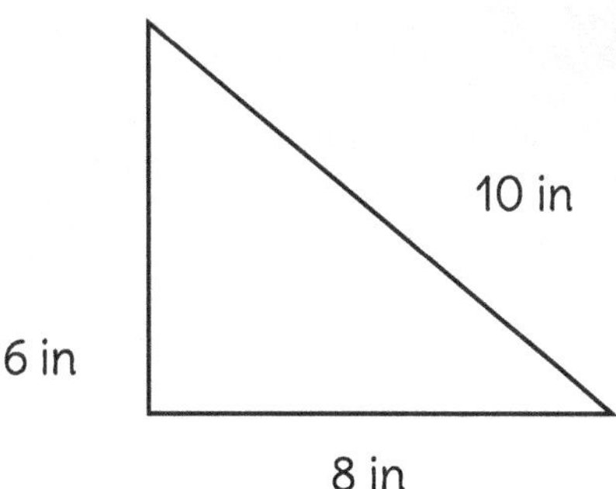

$$A = \frac{1}{2} \times \text{base} \times \text{height}$$

$$A = \frac{1}{2} \times 6 \times 8$$

$$A = \frac{1}{2} \times 48$$

$$A = 24$$

Perimeter of Triangle:

The perimeter of a triangle is the total length of its three sides. To find the perimeter, we simply add the lengths of all three sides together:

$$P = \text{side1} + \text{side2} + \text{side3}$$

$$P = 6 + 8 + 10$$

$$P = 24$$

Equilateral Triangle

An equilateral triangle is a triangle in which all three sides are equal in length. To find the area and perimeter of an equilateral triangle, we can use the following formulas:

- Area (A): $\frac{\sqrt{3}}{4} \times a^2$ where a is the length of one side of the equilateral triangle.
- Perimeter (P): $P = 3a$ where a is the length of one side of the equilateral triangle.

Area of Equilateral Triangle:

$$\text{Area (A): } \frac{\sqrt{3}}{4} \times (6)^2$$

$$\text{Area (A): } \frac{\sqrt{3}}{4} \times 36$$

$$\text{Area (A): } \frac{36\sqrt{3}}{4}$$

$$\text{Area (A): } \frac{36(1.73)}{4}$$

$$\text{Area (A): } \frac{62.35}{4}$$

$$\text{Area (A): } 15.59 \text{ in}^2$$

Perimeter of Equilateral Triangle:

$$P = 3a$$

$$P = 3(6) = 18$$

Isosceles Triangle

An isosceles triangle is a triangle with at least two sides of equal length. The angles opposite the equal sides are also equal.

Area of Isosceles Triangle

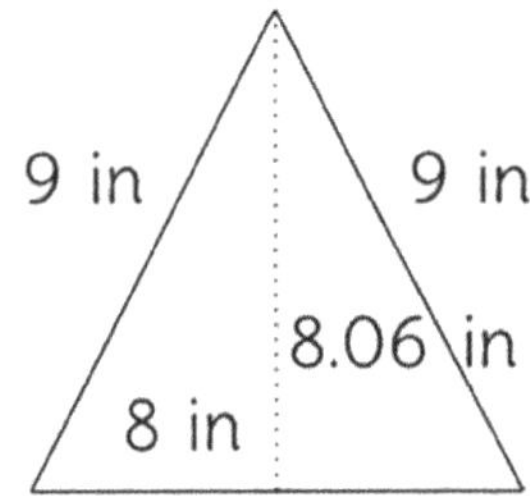

$$A = \frac{1}{2} \times \text{base} \times \text{height}$$

$$A = \frac{1}{2} \times 8 \times 8$$

$$A = \frac{1}{2} \times 64$$

$$A = 32$$

Perimeter of Isosceles Triangle

The perimeter of a triangle is the total length of its three sides. To find the perimeter, we simply add the lengths of all three sides together:

$$P = \text{side1} + \text{side2} + \text{side3}$$

$$P = 9 + 9 + 8$$

$$P = 26$$

Area and Circumference of circles

To find the area (A) and circumference (C) of a circle, we use the following formulas:

1. **Area of a Circle (A)** = $\pi \times (radius)^2$

- where π (pi) is a constant with value of (3.14). It is a ratio of the circumference of a circle to its diameter,
- the radius (r) is the distance from the center of the circle.

2. **Circumference of a Circle (C) = $2 \times \pi \times radius$**

Let's solve an example: suppose a swimming pool has a radius of 11 meters, we are required to calculate its Area and Circumference:

$$\text{Area } (A) = \pi \times (radius)^2$$

$$A = 3.14 \times 11^2$$

$$A = 3.14 \times 121$$

$$A = 379.94 \text{ square meters}$$

$$\text{Circumference } (C) = 2 \times \pi \times radius$$

$$C = 2 \times 3.14 \times 11$$

$$C = 69.08 \text{ square meters}$$

Unit Conversion

Metric Conversion
1 meter (m) = 100 centimeters (cm)
1 meter (m) = 1000 millimeters (mm)
1 kilometer (km) = 1000 meters (m)
1 hectare (ha) = 10000 square meters (m^2)
1 square meter (m^2) = 10000 square centimeters (cm^2)
1 cubic meter (m^3) = 1000 liters (L)

Weights and Measures
1 kilogram (kg) = 1000 grams (g)
1 liter (L) = 1000 milliliters (mL)
1 tonne (t) = 1000 kilograms (kg)
1 centimeter (cm) = 10 millimeters (mm)
1 gram (g) = 1000 milligrams (mg)
1 kilometer (km) = 100000 centimeters (cm)

Multiplication: (3 x 3)

Find the product.

1) 188
× 794

2) 274
× 158

3) 764
× 596

4) 274
× 334

5) 554
× 591

6) 846
× 386

7) 525
× 237

8) 786
× 184

9) 570
× 736

10) 489
  × 444
_____

11) 291
  × 945
_____

12) 553
  × 208
_____

13) 131
  × 382
_____

14) 791
  × 755
_____

15) 244
  × 905
_____

16) 184
  × 663
_____

17) 602
  × 183
_____

18) 365
  × 446
_____

19) $\begin{array}{r} 607 \\ \times\ 721 \\ \hline \end{array}$	**20)** $\begin{array}{r} 264 \\ \times\ 222 \\ \hline \end{array}$	**21)** $\begin{array}{r} 149 \\ \times\ 732 \\ \hline \end{array}$
22) $\begin{array}{r} 538 \\ \times\ 483 \\ \hline \end{array}$	**23)** $\begin{array}{r} 160 \\ \times\ 943 \\ \hline \end{array}$	**24)** $\begin{array}{r} 879 \\ \times\ 649 \\ \hline \end{array}$
25) $\begin{array}{r} 718 \\ \times\ 110 \\ \hline \end{array}$	**26)** $\begin{array}{r} 642 \\ \times\ 987 \\ \hline \end{array}$	**27)** $\begin{array}{r} 895 \\ \times\ 784 \\ \hline \end{array}$

Multi Digit Multiplication

Find the product.

1)	1,660 × 243		**2)**	3,418 × 166	**3)**	1,274 × 483
4)	8,047 × 519		**5)**	1,896 × 647	**6)**	5,077 × 282
7)	7,847 × 442		**8)**	8,715 × 439	**9)**	5,771 × 848

10) 5,730
   × 367

11) 3,958
   × 558

12) 5,073
   × 170

13) 1,487
   × 187

14) 5,016
   × 243

15) 1,370
   × 235

16) 3,633
   × 196

17) 7,676
   × 817

18) 1,172
   × 223

19)	2,047 × 541	**20)**	6,942 × 780	**21)**	4,169 × 629
22)	6,429 × 889	**23)**	9,756 × 877	**24)**	2,587 × 538
25)	7,775 × 378	**26)**	5,327 × 793	**27)**	5,147 × 628

Long Division

Find the quotient.

1)

$$4\overline{)88{,}619}$$

2)

$$4\overline{)25{,}439}$$

3)

$$10\overline{)27{,}419}$$

4)

$$5\overline{)50{,}609}$$

5)

$$8\overline{)65{,}908}$$

6)

$$7\overline{)71{,}744}$$

7)

$$5\overline{)39{,}638}$$

8)

$$10\overline{)94{,}825}$$

9)

$$3\overline{)65{,}969}$$

10)

$$7\overline{)82{,}198}$$

11)

$$10\overline{)42{,}886}$$

12)

$$7\overline{)56{,}546}$$

13)

9⟌96,640

14)

5⟌16,732

15)

4⟌35,433

16)

8⟌78,669

17)

9⟌40,022

18)

6⟌85,325

19)

$$3 \overline{)18{,}782}$$

20)

$$7 \overline{)21{,}723}$$

21)

$$4 \overline{)63{,}329}$$

22)

$$7 \overline{)94{,}677}$$

23)

$$8 \overline{)71{,}802}$$

24)

$$3 \overline{)16{,}276}$$

25)

$$8\overline{)94{,}367}$$

26)

$$4\overline{)80{,}825}$$

27)

$$8\overline{)98{,}726}$$

28)

$$9\overline{)26{,}597}$$

29)

$$6\overline{)81{,}402}$$

30)

$$5\overline{)35{,}921}$$

Long Division: Remainders

Find the quotient.

1)

$$18\overline{)33{,}583}$$

2)

$$15\overline{)48{,}715}$$

3)

$$14\overline{)16{,}388}$$

4)

$$6\overline{)70{,}784}$$

5)

$$10 \overline{)48{,}247}$$

6)

$$12 \overline{)54{,}211}$$

7)

$$6 \overline{)62{,}466}$$

8)

$$10 \overline{)95{,}181}$$

9)

$$12\overline{)53{,}321}$$

10)

$$16\overline{)33{,}212}$$

11)

$$9\overline{)66{,}391}$$

12)

$$9\overline{)29{,}184}$$

13)

$$10\overline{)85{,}814}$$

14)

$$10\overline{)80{,}258}$$

15)

$$4\overline{)43{,}636}$$

16)

$$10\overline{)65{,}197}$$

17)

$$18\overline{)69{,}756}$$

18)

$$11\overline{)69{,}108}$$

19)

$$18\overline{)99{,}137}$$

20)

$$16\overline{)75{,}385}$$

Multiplying Decimals

Find the product.

1)
```
   53.19
×   1.85
```

2)
```
   86.10
×   7.71
```

3)
```
   91.87
×   7.24
```

4)
```
   96.79
×   6.33
```

5)
```
   38.99
×   3.37
```

6)
```
   88.63
×   1.24
```

7)
```
   29.50
×   9.95
```

8)
```
   78.41
×   8.74
```

9)
```
   69.36
×   1.45
```

10)   87.79
   ×   6.74

11)   89.52
   ×   3.26

12)   84.58
   ×   3.95

13)   82.74
   ×   1.65

14)   88.41
   ×   7.18

15)   62.81
   ×   4.85

16)   49.61
   ×   6.39

17)   84.14
   ×   5.10

18)   35.44
   ×   5.79

19)
$$59.95 \times 5.20$$

20)
$$52.32 \times 2.33$$

21)
$$52.13 \times 2.69$$

22)
$$19.20 \times 1.99$$

23)
$$30.10 \times 6.28$$

24)
$$28.20 \times 7.01$$

25)
$$22.15 \times 8.15$$

26)
$$87.23 \times 9.45$$

27)
$$11.53 \times 1.79$$

28)	92.60 × 3.06	29)	33.88 × 5.65	30)	94.41 × 8.53
31)	84.08 × 3.49	32)	10.51 × 9.03	33)	84.10 × 3.46
34)	28.22 × 7.84	35)	74.17 × 3.05	36)	37.57 × 2.73

Dividing Decimals

Find the quotient.

1)

$1.3\overline{)88.0}$

2)

$1.5\overline{)70.8}$

3)

$1.3\overline{)96.0}$

4)

$1.4\overline{)37.9}$

5)

$1.4\overline{)17.0}$

6)

$1.8\overline{)38.9}$

7)

$1.9\overline{)87.7}$

8)

$1.9\overline{)38.8}$

9)

$1.7\overline{)19.4}$

10)

$$1.9\overline{)34.9}$$

11)

$$1.4\overline{)42.5}$$

12)

$$1.3\overline{)20.0}$$

13)

$$1.4\overline{)66.7}$$

14)

$$1.2\overline{)30.5}$$

15)

$$1.6\overline{)88.9}$$

16)

$$1.2\overline{)92.5}$$

17)

$$1.6\overline{)57.1}$$

18)

$$1.1\overline{)35.6}$$

19)

$1.2\overline{)78.9}$

20)

$1.7\overline{)10.3}$

21)

$1.4\overline{)69.5}$

22)

$1.6\overline{)85.0}$

23)

$1.2\overline{)91.4}$

24)

$1.9\overline{)51.1}$

25)

$1.2\overline{)26.1}$

26)

$1.4\overline{)68.9}$

27)

$1.3\overline{)11.6}$

28)

$$1.4\overline{)65.2}$$

29)

$$1.4\overline{)27.6}$$

30)

$$1.6\overline{)88.2}$$

31)

$$1.2\overline{)18.1}$$

32)

$$1.5\overline{)60.4}$$

33)

$$1.1\overline{)52.3}$$

34)

$$1.2\overline{)31.2}$$

35)

$$1.2\overline{)63.7}$$

36)

$$1.9\overline{)18.1}$$

The Power of 10

1)

$$10\overline{)27}$$

2)

$$\begin{array}{r} 88 \\ \times\ 100 \\ \hline \end{array}$$

3)

$$100\overline{)96}$$

4)

$$10\overline{)86}$$

5)

$$10\overline{)11}$$

6)

$$\begin{array}{r} 29 \\ \times\ 10 \\ \hline \end{array}$$

7)

$$100\overline{)60}$$

8)

$$10\overline{)17}$$

9)

$$\begin{array}{r} 31 \\ \times\ 10 \\ \hline \end{array}$$

10)

$$100\overline{)66}$$

11)

$$100\overline{)93}$$

12)

$$\begin{array}{r} 48 \\ \times\ 100 \\ \hline \end{array}$$

13)

$$\begin{array}{r} 98 \\ \times\ 10 \\ \hline \end{array}$$

14)

$$\begin{array}{r} 48 \\ \times\ 1,000 \\ \hline \end{array}$$

15)

$$\begin{array}{r} 26 \\ \times\ 10 \\ \hline \end{array}$$

16)

$$\begin{array}{r} 97 \\ \times\ 10 \\ \hline \end{array}$$

17)
$$32 \times 10$$

18)
$$10\overline{)16}$$

19)
$$51 \times 100$$

20)
$$38 \times 100$$

21)
$$74 \times 10$$

22)
$$1{,}000\overline{)30}$$

23)
$$67 \times 10$$

24)
$$1{,}000\overline{)22}$$

25)
$$10\overline{)18}$$

26)
$$100\overline{)17}$$

27)
$$100\overline{)76}$$

28)
$$82 \times 10$$

29)
$$1{,}000\overline{)66}$$

30)
$$64 \times 1{,}000$$

31)
$$68 \times 1{,}000$$

32)
$$10\overline{)20}$$

Place Value

Determine the place value of the underlined digit.

1) 9,543,709.5 = _______________________

2) 815,486.48 = _______________________

3) 233,153.48 = _______________________

4) 157,535.2 = _______________________

5) 241,405.2 = _______________________

6) 27,026.205 = _______________________

7) 21,748,449 = _______________________

8) 44,69_1_,518 = _______________________

9) 73,_4_77,232 = _______________________

10) 44,_8_61,161 = _______________________

11) 22,56_7_.936 = _______________________

12) 9_6_,452.659 = _______________________

13) 34,_9_91.259 = _______________________

14) _8_,421,444 = _______________________

15) 68,01_8_.075 = _______________________

16) 4<u>2</u>0,077.57 = _______________________________

17) 539,069.<u>4</u>4 = _______________________________

18) 21,<u>5</u>32.502 = _______________________________

19) 48,2<u>0</u>1,801 = _______________________________

20) 3<u>5</u>0,385.22 = _______________________________

21) 15,435,85<u>6</u> = _______________________________

22) 487,729.<u>7</u> = _______________________________

23) 463,408.0<u>1</u> = _______________________________

24) 97,281,510 = _______________________________

25) 31,212,695 = _______________________________

26) 8,530,919.5 = _______________________________

27) 78,100,344 = _______________________________

28) 93,956.403 = _______________________________

29) 531,328.58 = _______________________________

30) 777,580.44 = _______________________________

31) 50,032.692 = _______________________________

32) 6,683,0<u>8</u>5 = _______________________________

33) 987,2<u>3</u>7.64 = _______________________________

34) 83,708.14<u>2</u> = _______________________________

35) 527,<u>0</u>87.56 = _______________________________

36) 27,6<u>0</u>9,907 = _______________________________

37) 3,49<u>7</u>,114.9 = _______________________________

38) 208,064.1<u>3</u> = _______________________________

39) 8,36<u>8</u>,984.7 = _______________________________

Place Value and Expanded Notation

1) ______________________________

6 ten thousands + 5 thousands + 3 hundreds + 8 tens + 4 ones + 3 tenths + 3 hundredths + 4 thousandths

2) ______________________________

7 hundred thousands + 8 ten thousands + 8 thousands + 7 hundreds + 6 tens + 4 ones + 3 tenths + 1 hundredth

3) ______________________________

9 hundred thousands + 6 ten thousands + 4 hundreds + 4 tens + 6 ones + 3 tenths + 1 hundredth

4) ______________________________

8 ten millions + 2 millions + 4 hundred thousands + 2 thousands + 5 tens + 9 ones

5) _______________________

1 million + 8 hundred thousands + 9 ten thousands + 3 thousands + 7 hundreds + 3 tens + 1 one + 2 tenths

6) _______________________

3 hundred thousands + 6 ten thousands + 2 thousands + 6 hundreds + 5 tens + 5 ones + 8 tenths + 8 hundredths

7) _______________________

5 millions + 4 hundred thousands + 8 ten thousands + 5 thousands + 8 hundreds + 5 tens + 2 ones + 3 tenths

8) _______________________

6 millions + 5 hundred thousands + 7 ten thousands + 9 thousands + 5 hundreds + 8 tens + 7 ones + 9 tenths

9) ___________________________

7 ten millions + 6 millions + 9 hundred thousands + 4 ten thousands + 3 thousands + 3 hundreds + 1 ten + 8 ones

10) ___________________________

2 ten thousands + 5 thousands + 5 hundreds + 5 tens + 8 ones + 2 tenths + 9 hundredths

11) ___________________________

6 millions + 8 hundred thousands + 8 ten thousands + 1 thousand + 8 hundreds + 7 tens + 8 ones + 7 tenths

12) ___________________________

4 ten thousands + 5 thousands + 9 tens + 6 ones + 2 tenths + 5 hundredths + 1 thousandth

13) _______________________

6 millions + 1 hundred thousand + 5 ten thousands + 5 thousands + 4 hundreds + 8 tens + 7 ones + 2 tenths

14) _______________________

7 ten thousands + 3 thousands + 8 hundreds + 9 tens + 7 ones + 3 tenths + 6 hundredths + 2 thousandths

15) _______________________

4 millions + 5 hundred thousands + 8 ten thousands + 6 thousands + 1 hundred + 1 ten + 8 ones + 3 tenths

16) _______________________

9 ten thousands + 2 thousands + 7 hundreds + 4 tens + 1 one + 3 thousandths

17) _______________________ 9 ten millions + 9 millions + 6 ten thousands + 5 thousands + 1 hundred + 5 tens + 1 one

18) _______________________ 3 hundred thousands + 7 ten thousands + 4 thousands + 1 ten + 1 one + 5 tenths + 1 hundredth

19) _______________________ 9 hundred thousands + 5 ten thousands + 8 thousands + 5 hundreds + 3 tens + 9 ones + 6 tenths + 5 hundredths

20) _______________________ 2 millions + 7 hundred thousands + 3 ten thousands + 6 thousands + 2 hundreds + 3 tens + 9 ones + 9 tenths

21) ______________________________

8 ten thousands + 2 thousands + 7 hundreds + 6 tens + 2 ones + 6 tenths + 3 hundredths + 4 thousandths

22) ______________________________

1 million + 3 hundred thousands + 3 thousands + 6 hundreds + 2 tens + 7 ones + 2 tenths

23) ______________________________

1 million + 6 hundred thousands + 5 ten thousands + 1 thousand + 2 hundreds + 8 tens + 4 tenths

24) ______________________________

7 millions + 2 hundred thousands + 4 ten thousands + 2 thousands + 9 hundreds + 1 ten + 2 ones + 9 tenths

25) ______________________ 3 ten millions + 8 millions + 7 hundred thousands + 9 ten thousands + 1 thousand + 7 hundreds + 6 tens + 6 ones

26) ______________________ 3 hundred thousands + 6 ten thousands + 4 hundreds + 4 tens + 2 ones + 8 tenths + 4 hundredths

27) ______________________ 3 ten millions + 4 millions + 9 hundred thousands + 5 ten thousands + 4 thousands + 3 hundreds + 8 tens + 6 ones

28) ______________________ 4 ten millions + 6 hundred thousands + 6 ten thousands + 6 thousands + 4 hundreds + 2 tens + 7 ones

Place Value and Expanded Notation

1) 95,072.203

2) 7,330,896.0

3) 82,863.560

4) 56,915.639

5) 10,000.829

6) 1,514,893.0

7) 423,445.60

8) 7,240,668.4

9) 45,461.052

10) 680,061.08

11) 98,099.296

12) 1,683,494.3

13) 8,298,413.0

14) 77,684.181

15) 6,335,984.0 ___________________________

____

____

16) 8,276,061.6 ___________________________

____

____

17) 2,541,620.7 ___________________________

____

____

18) 71,319,829 ___________________________

____

____

19) 384,346.80 ___________________________

____

____

20) 8,568,907.5

21) 623,037.13

22) 61,112.653

23) 55,417.932

24) 8,129,394.7

25) 52,949,581

26) 774,652.40

27) 678,255.19

28) 623,480.61

29) 7,236,362.7

Lowest Common Multiple

Find the lowest common multiple.

1) 5

2

2) 7

4

3) 6

4

4) 6

10

5) 8

3

6) 2
   5

7) 2
   3

8) 6
   2

9) 3
   7

10) 9
    5

11) 8
    2

12)   2
8

13)   3
8

14)   10
9

15)   4
9

16)   5
6

17)   9
7

18) 5
4

19) 4
8

20) 3
10

21) 8
7

22) 6
5

23) 7
10

24) 9
     4

25) 9
     2

26) 3
     6

27) 5
     7

28) 2
     7

29) 3
     9

Equivalent Fractions

1) $\dfrac{5}{7} = \dfrac{35}{}$

2) $\dfrac{13}{16} = \dfrac{}{144}$

3) $\dfrac{14}{15} = \dfrac{}{135}$

4) $\dfrac{}{9} = \dfrac{8}{18}$

5) $\dfrac{2}{8} = \dfrac{14}{}$

6) $\dfrac{13}{19} = \dfrac{78}{}$

7) $\dfrac{2}{3} = \dfrac{8}{}$

8) $\dfrac{2}{4} = \dfrac{10}{}$

9) $\dfrac{4}{} = \dfrac{40}{110}$

10) $\dfrac{6}{10} = \dfrac{}{90}$

11) $\dfrac{5}{20} = \dfrac{}{120}$

12) $\dfrac{}{12} = \dfrac{10}{120}$

13) $\dfrac{7}{} = \dfrac{28}{56}$

14) $\dfrac{}{18} = \dfrac{50}{180}$

15) $\dfrac{4}{} = \dfrac{20}{25}$

16) $\dfrac{12}{13} = \dfrac{}{65}$

17) $\dfrac{8}{15} = \dfrac{}{75}$

18) $\dfrac{}{19} = \dfrac{48}{114}$

19) $\dfrac{}{11} = \dfrac{49}{77}$

20) $\dfrac{2}{6} = \dfrac{10}{}$

21) $\dfrac{6}{} = \dfrac{60}{120}$

22) $\dfrac{}{2} = \dfrac{4}{8}$

Fractions Addition: Uncommon Denominator

Find the sum.

1) $\frac{5}{11} + \frac{1}{2} =$ _______________

2) $\frac{5}{9} + \frac{2}{10} =$ _______________

3) $\frac{8}{11} + \frac{1}{16} =$ _______________

4) $\frac{3}{14} + \frac{3}{13} =$ _______________

5) $\frac{1}{4} + \frac{2}{12} =$ _______________

6) $\frac{1}{3} + \frac{6}{19} =$ _______________

7) $\frac{6}{16} + \frac{1}{20} =$ _______________

8) $\frac{3}{10} + \frac{4}{8} =$ _______________

9) $\frac{1}{12} + \frac{2}{15} =$ _______________

10) $\frac{14}{20} + \frac{1}{6} =$ _______________

11) $\frac{1}{2} + \frac{3}{17} =$ _______________

12) $\frac{1}{16} + \frac{5}{8} =$ _______________

13) $\dfrac{1}{12} + \dfrac{15}{17} =$ _________________

14) $\dfrac{2}{3} + \dfrac{3}{14} =$ _________________

15) $\dfrac{1}{2} + \dfrac{1}{2} =$ _________________

16) $\dfrac{13}{20} + \dfrac{1}{7} =$ _________________

17) $\dfrac{5}{15} + \dfrac{3}{6} =$ _________________

18) $\dfrac{7}{14} + \dfrac{2}{19} =$ _________________

19) $\dfrac{1}{4} + \dfrac{9}{20} =$ _________________

20) $\dfrac{3}{5} + \dfrac{2}{12} =$ _________________

21) $\dfrac{7}{11} + \dfrac{1}{3} =$ _________________

22) $\dfrac{1}{4} + \dfrac{2}{8} =$ _________________

23) $\dfrac{3}{8} + \dfrac{4}{9} =$ _________________

24) $\dfrac{2}{14} + \dfrac{9}{20} =$ _________________

25) $\dfrac{2}{9} + \dfrac{2}{10} =$ _______________

26) $\dfrac{2}{5} + \dfrac{2}{4} =$ _______________

27) $\dfrac{3}{17} + \dfrac{2}{13} =$ _______________

28) $\dfrac{1}{2} + \dfrac{2}{17} =$ _______________

29) $\dfrac{1}{10} + \dfrac{7}{19} =$ _______________

30) $\dfrac{2}{11} + \dfrac{1}{12} =$ _______________

31) $\dfrac{1}{13} + \dfrac{1}{10} =$ _______________

32) $\dfrac{2}{7} + \dfrac{1}{2} =$ _______________

33) $\dfrac{2}{10} + \dfrac{1}{3} =$ _______________

34) $\dfrac{1}{5} + \dfrac{2}{8} =$ _______________

35) $\dfrac{7}{9} + \dfrac{1}{13} =$ _______________

36) $\dfrac{4}{14} + \dfrac{1}{4} =$ _______________

Fractions Subtraction: (Uncommon Denominator)

Find the difference.

1) $\dfrac{7}{8} - \dfrac{9}{18} =$ ___________________

2) $\dfrac{7}{13} - \dfrac{5}{10} =$ ___________________

3) $\dfrac{6}{10} - \dfrac{6}{11} =$ ___________________

4) $\dfrac{13}{18} - \dfrac{4}{9} =$ ___________________

5) $\dfrac{14}{19} - \dfrac{9}{16} =$ ___________________

6) $\dfrac{11}{13} - \dfrac{8}{10} =$ ___________________

7) $\dfrac{14}{20} - \dfrac{4}{20} =$ ___________________

8) $\dfrac{10}{16} - \dfrac{3}{5} =$ ___________________

9) $\dfrac{8}{17} - \dfrac{4}{9} =$ ___________________

10) $\dfrac{2}{3} - \dfrac{1}{15} =$ ___________________

11) $\dfrac{1}{2} - \dfrac{7}{17} =$ ___________________

12) $\dfrac{16}{20} - \dfrac{1}{2} =$ ___________________

13) $\dfrac{9}{15} - \dfrac{2}{20} =$ _______________

14) $\dfrac{9}{13} - \dfrac{1}{19} =$ _______________

15) $\dfrac{8}{11} - \dfrac{1}{2} =$ _______________

16) $\dfrac{6}{9} - \dfrac{2}{15} =$ _______________

17) $\dfrac{9}{17} - \dfrac{1}{10} =$ _______________

18) $\dfrac{4}{19} - \dfrac{1}{9} =$ _______________

19) $\dfrac{10}{20} - \dfrac{1}{17} =$ _______________

20) $\dfrac{6}{10} - \dfrac{1}{2} =$ _______________

21) $\dfrac{9}{13} - \dfrac{4}{13} =$ _______________

22) $\dfrac{3}{5} - \dfrac{8}{20} =$ _______________

23) $\dfrac{10}{12} - \dfrac{3}{5} =$ _______________

24) $\dfrac{7}{13} - \dfrac{1}{11} =$ _______________

25) $\dfrac{7}{8} - \dfrac{1}{3} =$ _______________

26) $\dfrac{6}{7} - \dfrac{1}{9} =$ _______________

27) $\dfrac{3}{6} - \dfrac{1}{4} =$ _______________

28) $\dfrac{6}{8} - \dfrac{2}{5} =$ _______________

29) $\dfrac{13}{19} - \dfrac{2}{3} =$ _______________

30) $\dfrac{1}{2} - \dfrac{1}{4} =$ _______________

31) $\dfrac{14}{18} - \dfrac{2}{19} =$ _______________

32) $\dfrac{4}{6} - \dfrac{10}{20} =$ _______________

33) $\dfrac{9}{17} - \dfrac{3}{12} =$ _______________

34) $\dfrac{12}{16} - \dfrac{9}{14} =$ _______________

35) $\dfrac{6}{7} - \dfrac{5}{16} =$ _______________

36) $\dfrac{3}{6} - \dfrac{3}{8} =$ _______________

37) $\dfrac{3}{4} - \dfrac{1}{3} =$ _______________

38) $\dfrac{17}{20} - \dfrac{2}{4} =$ _______________

Fractions Multiplication

Find the product.

1) $\dfrac{1}{3} \times \dfrac{2}{9} =$ _______________

2) $\dfrac{10}{11} \times \dfrac{5}{8} =$ _______________

3) $\dfrac{4}{5} \times \dfrac{2}{3} =$ _______________

4) $\dfrac{1}{2} \times \dfrac{5}{7} =$ _______________

5) $\dfrac{1}{7} \times \dfrac{2}{11} =$ _______________

6) $\dfrac{3}{4} \times \dfrac{1}{2} =$ _______________

7) $\dfrac{2}{3} \times \dfrac{1}{2} =$ _______________

8) $\dfrac{1}{2} \times \dfrac{1}{5} =$ _______________

9) $\dfrac{8}{11} \times \dfrac{1}{4} =$ _______________

10) $\dfrac{3}{5} \times \dfrac{5}{8} =$ _______________

11) $\dfrac{1}{9} \times \dfrac{4}{9} =$ _______________

12) $\dfrac{1}{2} \times \dfrac{2}{3} =$ _______________

13) $\frac{1}{3} \times \frac{2}{5} =$ _______________

14) $\frac{1}{9} \times \frac{1}{4} =$ _______________

15) $\frac{1}{8} \times \frac{1}{2} =$ _______________

16) $\frac{6}{11} \times \frac{2}{3} =$ _______________

17) $\frac{5}{7} \times \frac{7}{12} =$ _______________

18) $\frac{1}{5} \times \frac{1}{4} =$ _______________

19) $\frac{1}{9} \times \frac{1}{2} =$ _______________

20) $\frac{6}{7} \times \frac{3}{4} =$ _______________

21) $\frac{1}{3} \times \frac{4}{5} =$ _______________

22) $\frac{1}{3} \times \frac{1}{3} =$ _______________

23) $\frac{1}{2} \times \frac{1}{7} =$ _______________

24) $\frac{2}{7} \times \frac{1}{2} =$ _______________

25) $\dfrac{7}{9} \times \dfrac{2}{3} =$ _______________

26) $\dfrac{4}{5} \times \dfrac{3}{4} =$ _______________

27) $\dfrac{1}{8} \times \dfrac{3}{11} =$ _______________

28) $\dfrac{4}{11} \times \dfrac{3}{4} =$ _______________

29) $\dfrac{7}{11} \times \dfrac{3}{10} =$ _______________

30) $\dfrac{2}{5} \times \dfrac{1}{2} =$ _______________

31) $\dfrac{1}{2} \times \dfrac{4}{9} =$ _______________

32) $\dfrac{1}{2} \times \dfrac{3}{4} =$ _______________

33) $\dfrac{2}{3} \times \dfrac{1}{5} =$ _______________

34) $\dfrac{1}{3} \times \dfrac{1}{5} =$ _______________

35) $\dfrac{3}{7} \times \dfrac{1}{2} =$ _______________

36) $\dfrac{1}{4} \times \dfrac{1}{3} =$ _______________

Fractions Division

Find the quotient.

1) $\frac{1}{3} \div \frac{6}{7} =$ _______________

2) $\frac{1}{2} \div \frac{1}{4} =$ _______________

3) $\frac{1}{6} \div \frac{1}{4} =$ _______________

4) $\frac{7}{12} \div \frac{2}{10} =$ _______________

5) $\frac{1}{2} \div \frac{5}{8} =$ _______________

6) $\frac{1}{3} \div \frac{1}{11} =$ _______________

7) $\frac{1}{4} \div \frac{3}{6} =$ _______________

8) $\frac{3}{5} \div \frac{6}{12} =$ _______________

9) $\frac{1}{4} \div \frac{1}{2} =$ _______________

10) $\frac{3}{8} \div \frac{7}{9} =$ _______________

11) $\frac{1}{11} \div \frac{3}{6} =$ _______________

12) $\frac{2}{5} \div \frac{3}{4} =$ _______________

13) $\dfrac{1}{6} \div \dfrac{1}{3} =$ _______________

14) $\dfrac{5}{7} \div \dfrac{6}{7} =$ _______________

15) $\dfrac{3}{5} \div \dfrac{1}{9} =$ _______________

16) $\dfrac{1}{7} \div \dfrac{1}{3} =$ _______________

17) $\dfrac{1}{2} \div \dfrac{2}{5} =$ _______________

18) $\dfrac{2}{3} \div \dfrac{1}{4} =$ _______________

19) $\dfrac{10}{11} \div \dfrac{2}{11} =$ _______________

20) $\dfrac{6}{11} \div \dfrac{5}{8} =$ _______________

21) $\dfrac{1}{6} \div \dfrac{3}{9} =$ _______________

22) $\dfrac{2}{5} \div \dfrac{5}{6} =$ _______________

23) $\dfrac{1}{3} \div \dfrac{1}{10} =$ _______________

24) $\dfrac{3}{8} \div \dfrac{10}{11} =$ _______________

25) $\dfrac{5}{6} \div \dfrac{9}{10} =$ _______________

26) $\dfrac{1}{2} \div \dfrac{3}{9} =$ _______________

27) $\dfrac{3}{11} \div \dfrac{1}{2} =$ _______________

28) $\dfrac{5}{9} \div \dfrac{2}{5} =$ _______________

29) $\dfrac{1}{8} \div \dfrac{5}{6} =$ _______________

30) $\dfrac{2}{9} \div \dfrac{7}{9} =$ _______________

31) $\dfrac{2}{5} \div \dfrac{1}{5} =$ _______________

32) $\dfrac{5}{9} \div \dfrac{10}{11} =$ _______________

33) $\dfrac{3}{10} \div \dfrac{2}{3} =$ _______________

34) $\dfrac{5}{7} \div \dfrac{4}{8} =$ _______________

35) $\dfrac{1}{3} \div \dfrac{1}{4} =$ _______________

36) $\dfrac{1}{2} \div \dfrac{2}{3} =$ _______________

Area and Perimeter

1)

2)

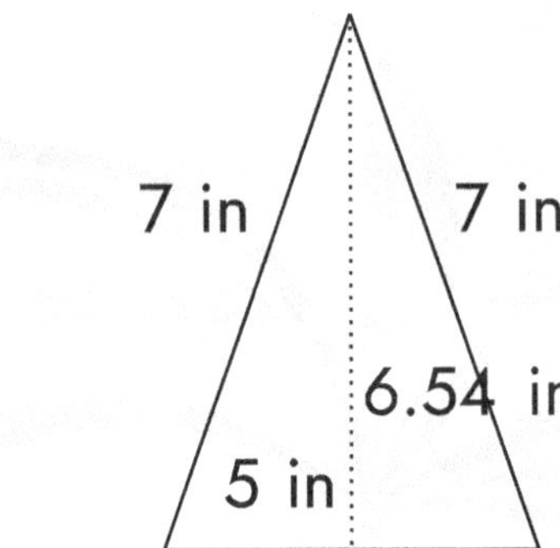

3)

4)

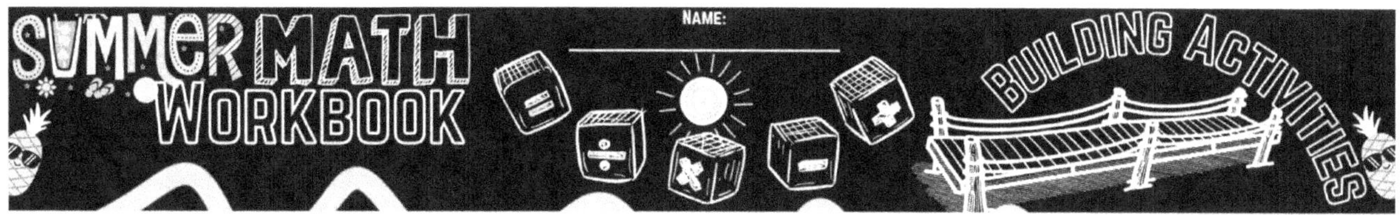

5)

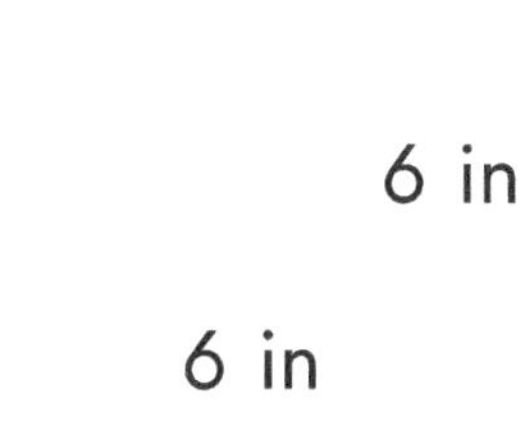

6)

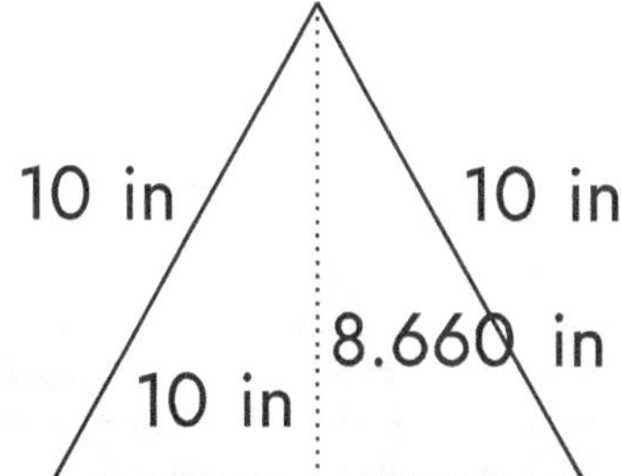

7)

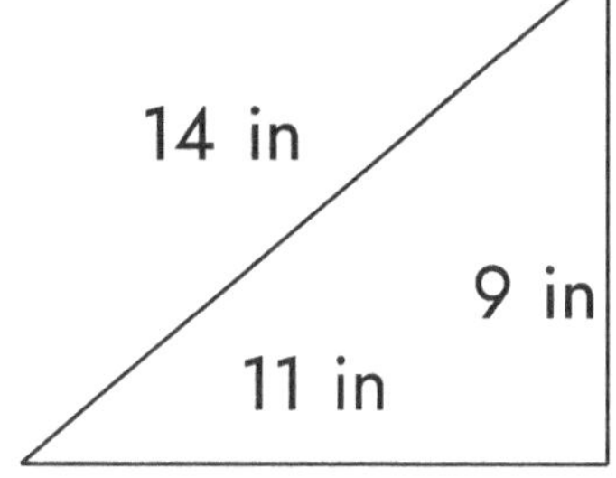

8)

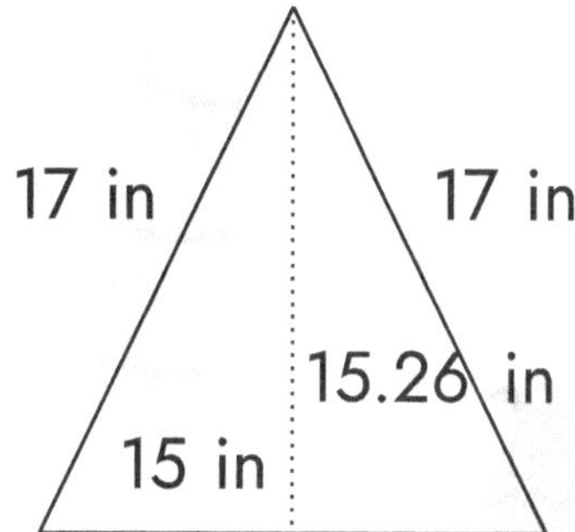

SUMMER MATH WORKBOOK
NAME:
BUILDING ACTIVITIES

9)

11 in
8 in
7 in

10)

9 in
9 in
9 in
7.794 in

11)

11 in
9 in
6 in

12)

8 in
8 in
6 in
7.42 in

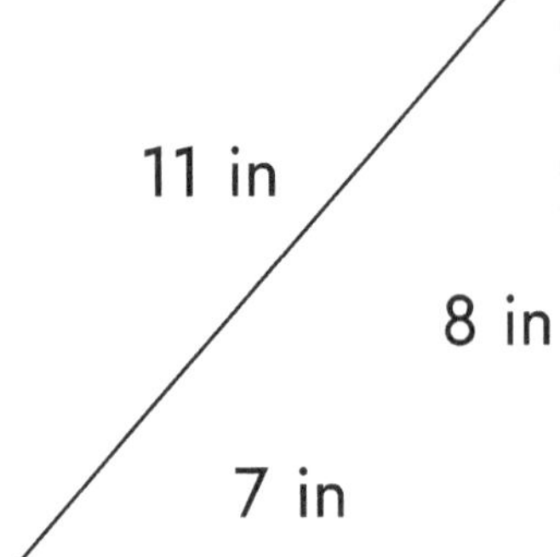

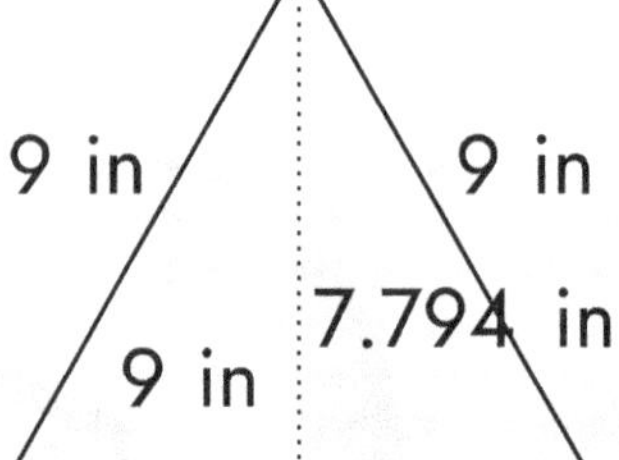

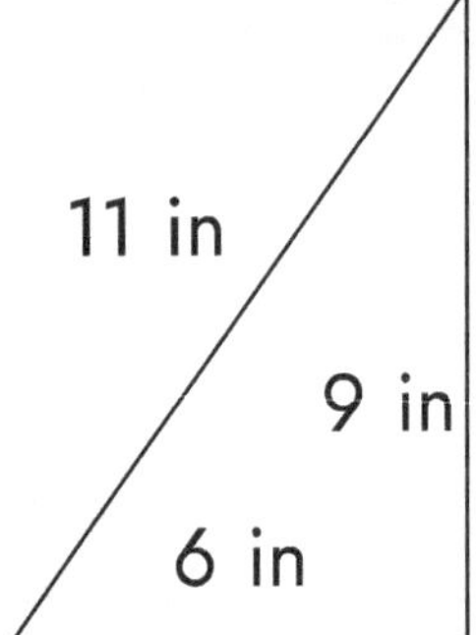

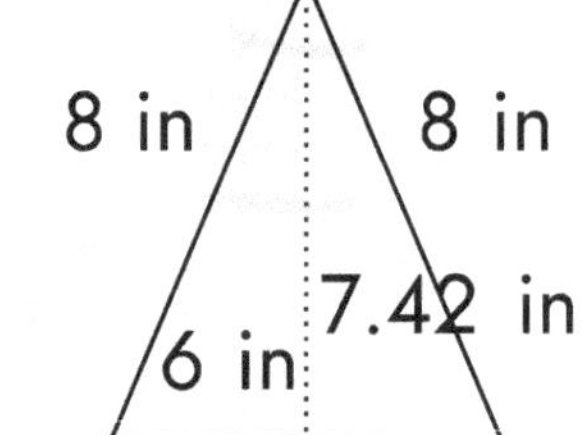

13)

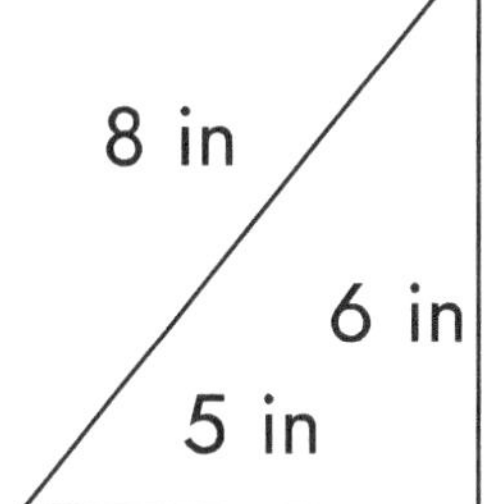

14)

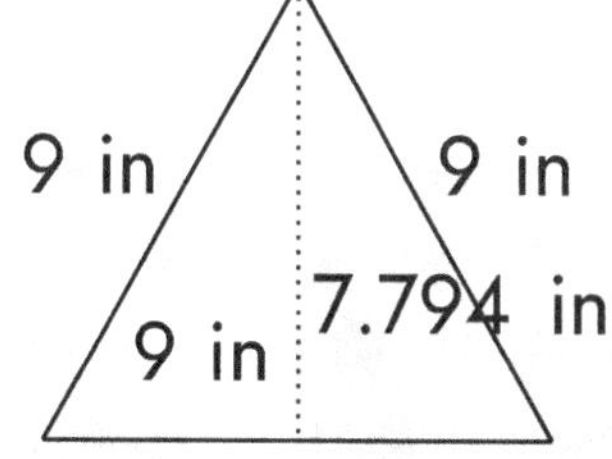

15)

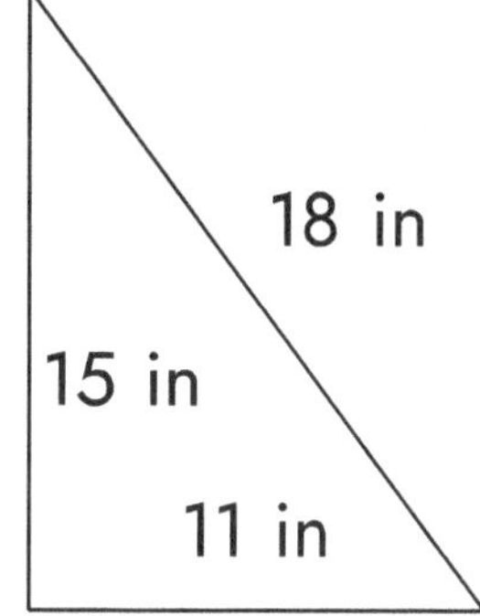

16)

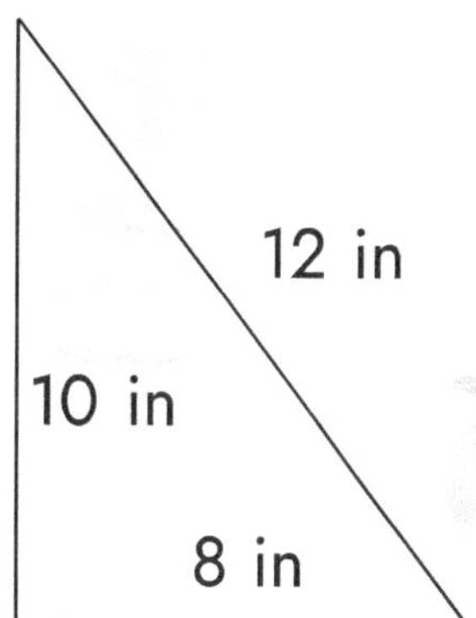

17)

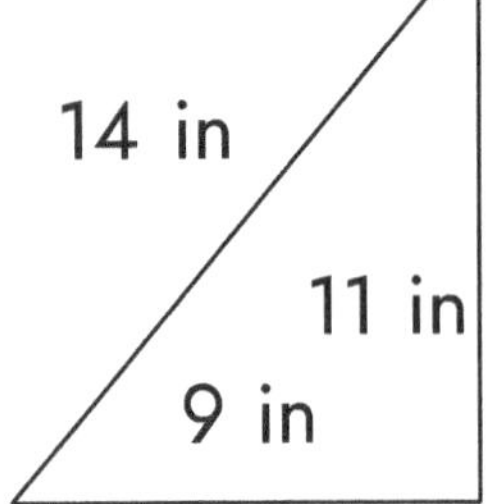

18)

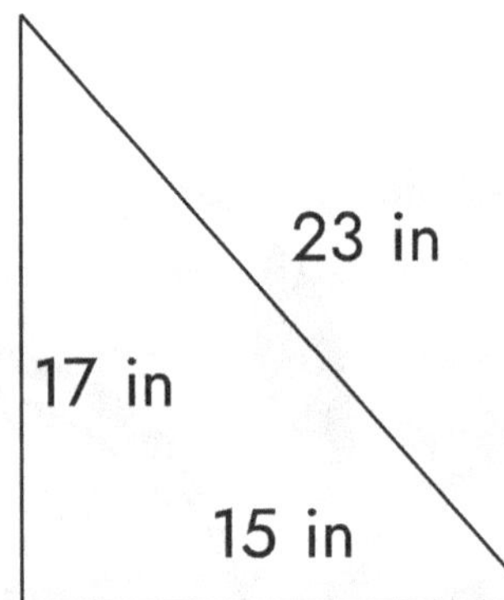

19)

20)

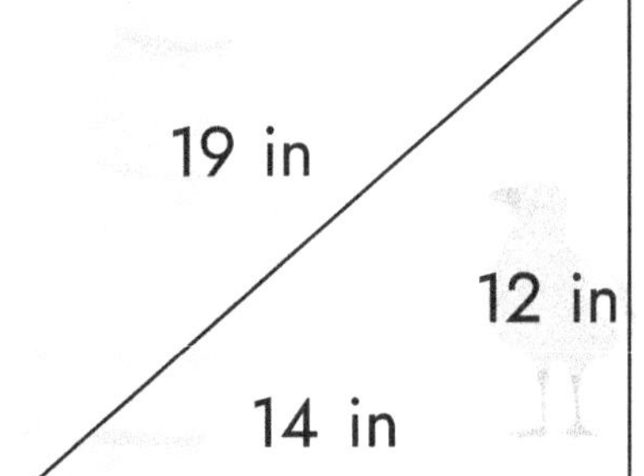

NAME:
SUMMER MATH WORKBOOK
BUILDING ACTIVITIES

21)

13 in
10 in

22)

8 in
8 in
7.60 in
5 in

23)

17 in
17 in
14.722 in
17 in

24)

11 in
11 in
9.526 in
11 in

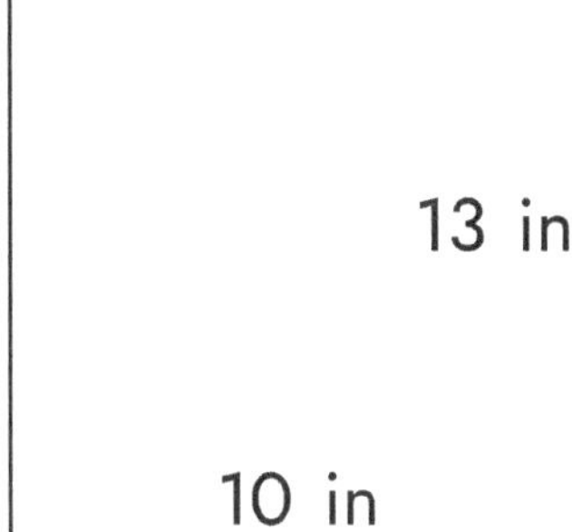

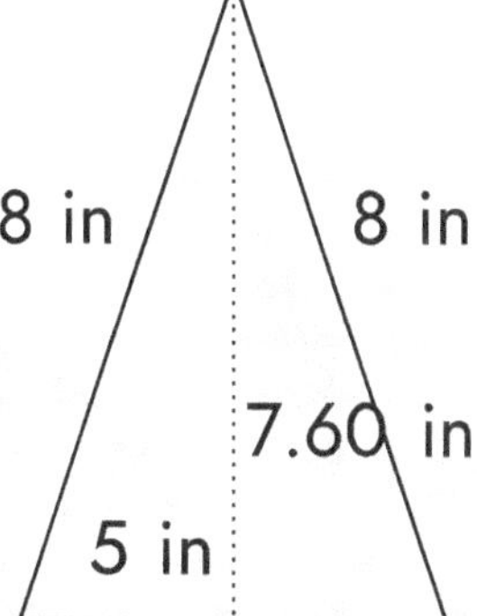

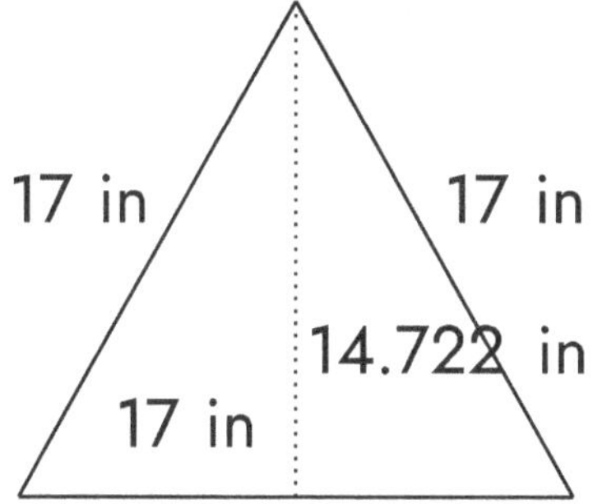

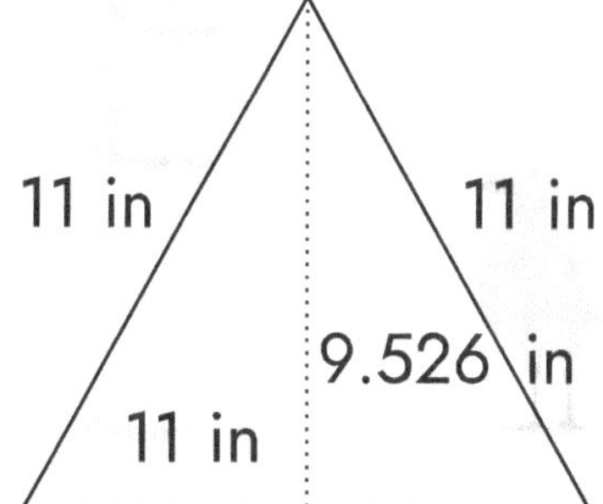

SUMMER MATH WORKBOOK
NAME:
BUILDING ACTIVITIES

25)

7 in
7 in
6.54 in
5 in

26)

9 in
9 in
8.29 in
7 in

27)

14 in
14 in
12.124 in
14 in

28)

9 in
9 in
8.29 in
7 in

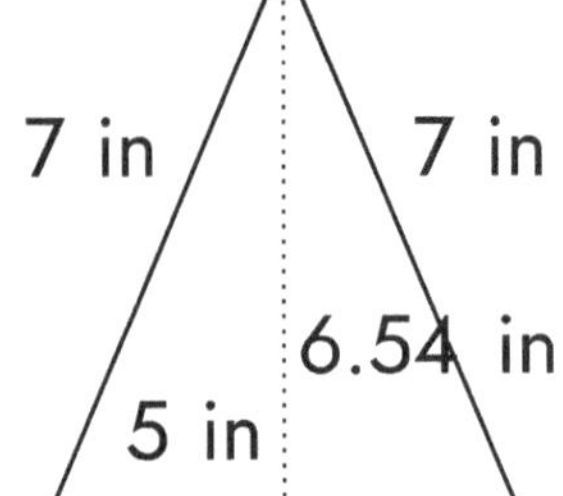

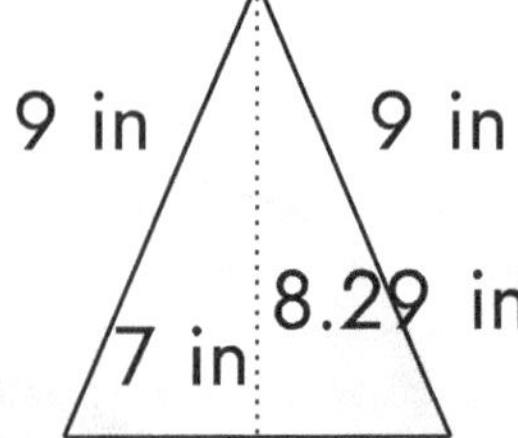

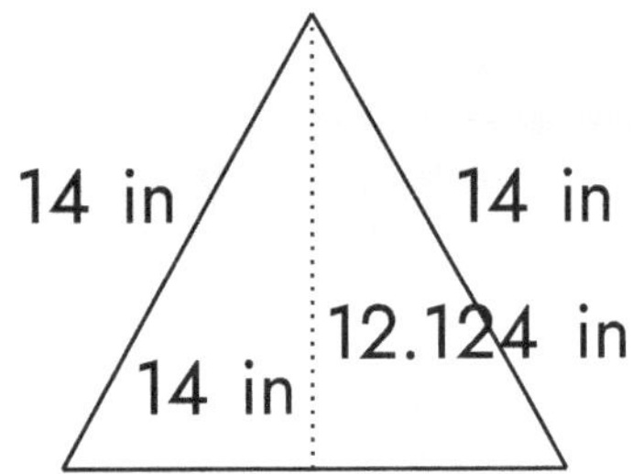

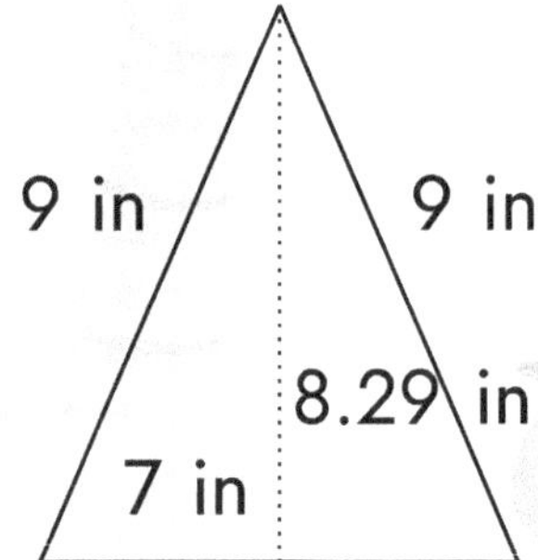

29)

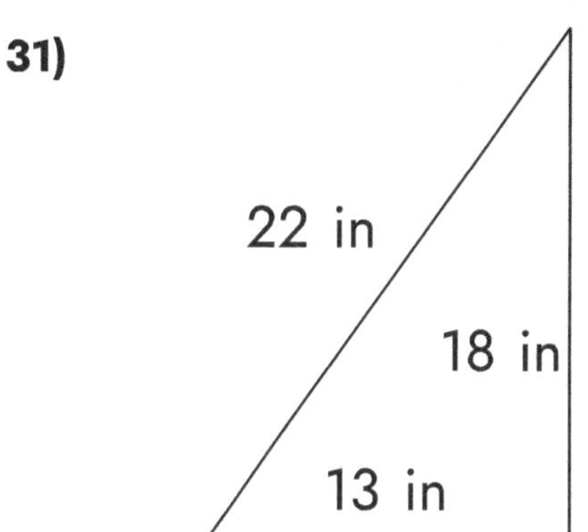

30)

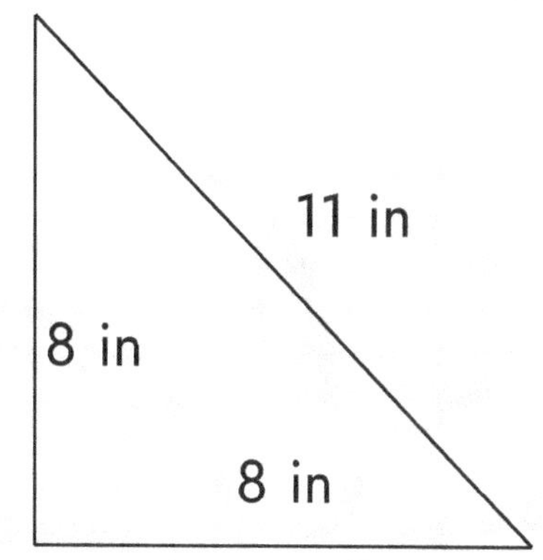

31)

32)

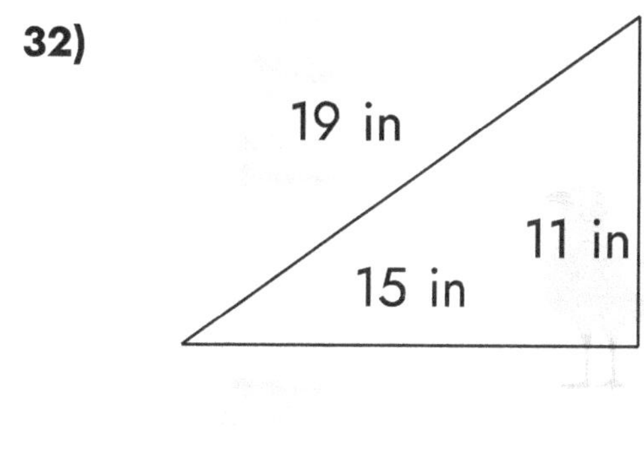

SUMMER MATH WORKBOOK
NAME:
BUILDING ACTIVITIES

33)

10 in
7 in
7 in

34)

11 in
8 in
8 in

35)

14 in
10 in
10 in

36)

15 in
12 in
10 in

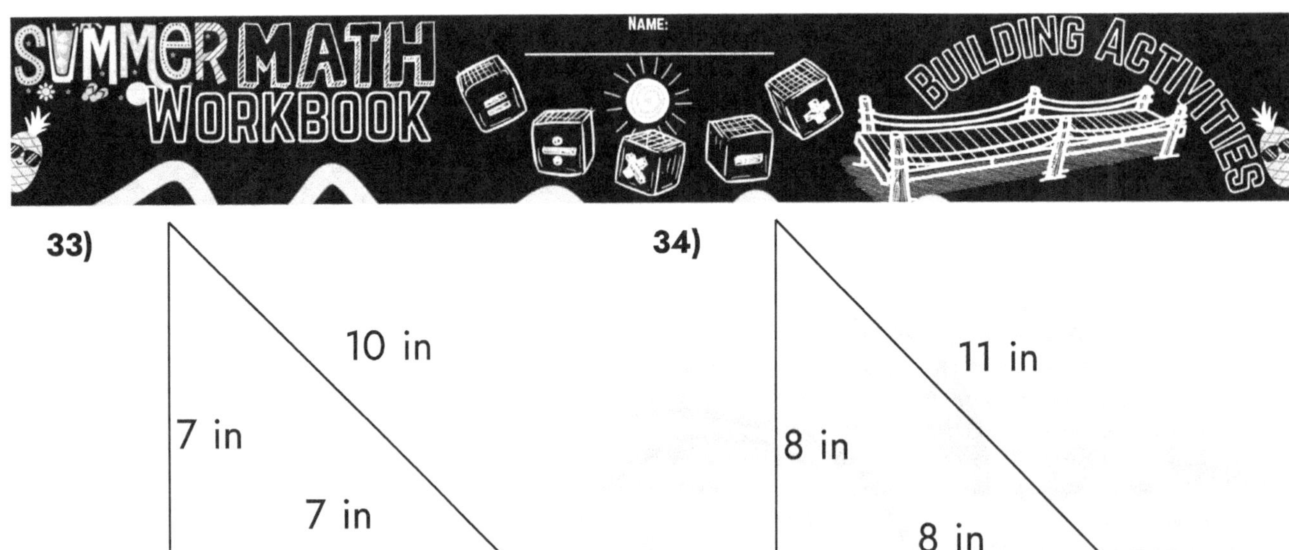

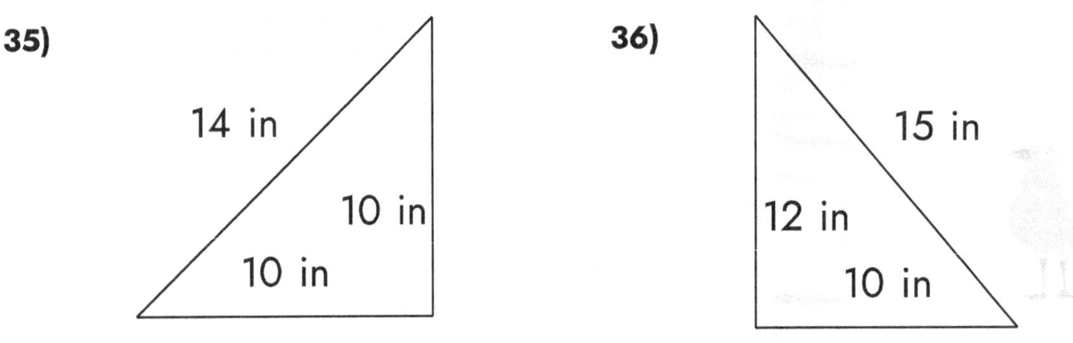

Area and Circumference

Calculate the area and circumference of each circle. Pi Value = 3.14

1)

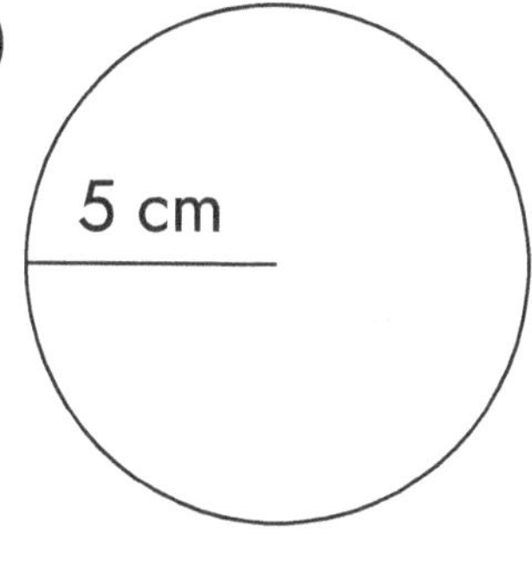

____

____

2)

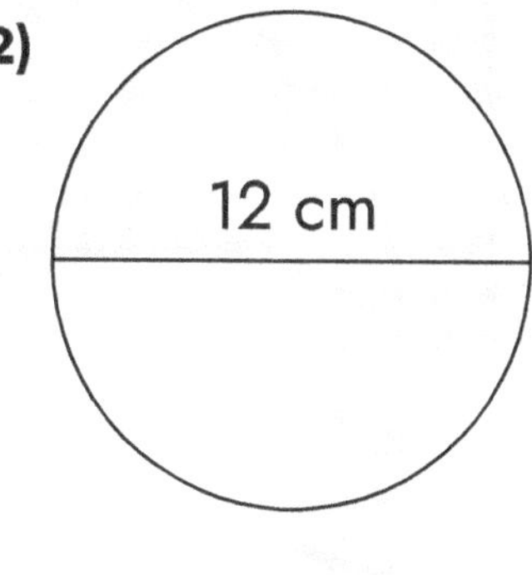

____

____

3)

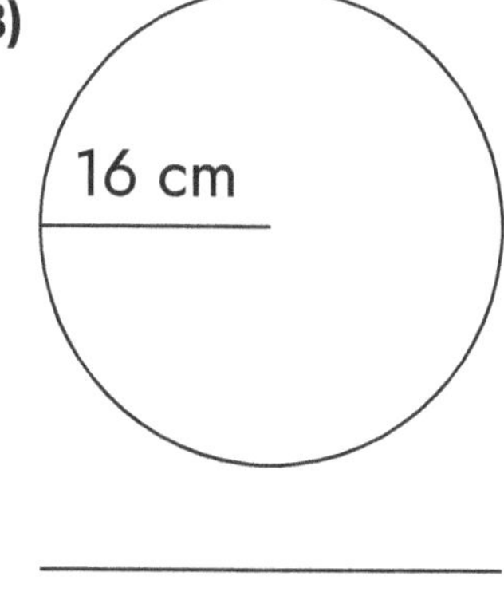

____

____

4)

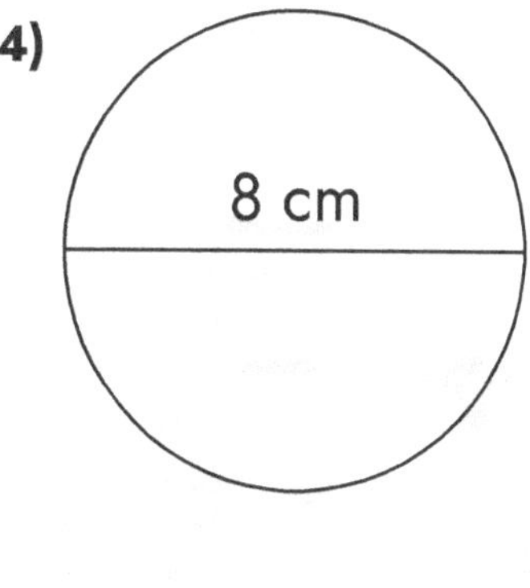

____

____

SUMMER MATH WORKBOOK
NAME:
BUILDING ACTIVITIES

5)

6 cm

____

____

6)

9 cm

____

____

7)

14 cm

____

____

8)

8 cm

____

____

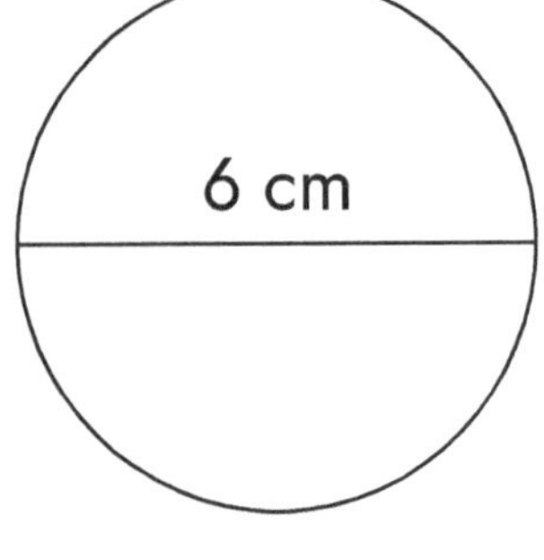

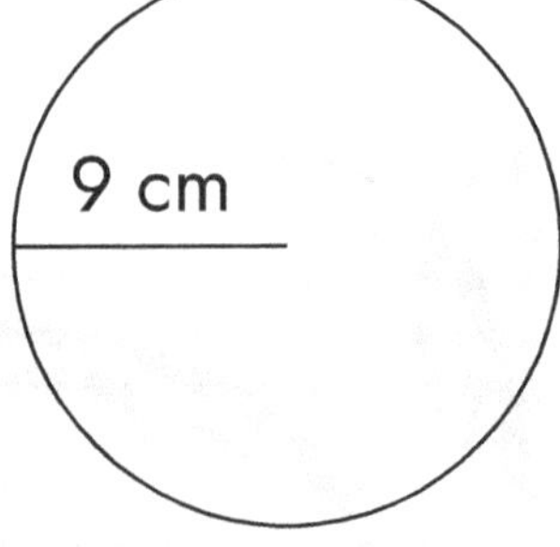

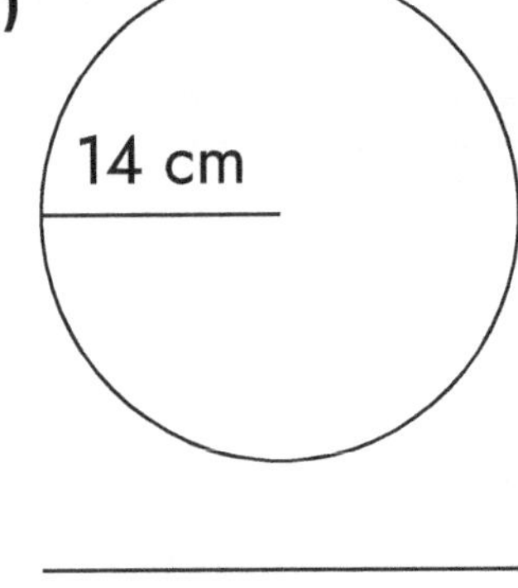

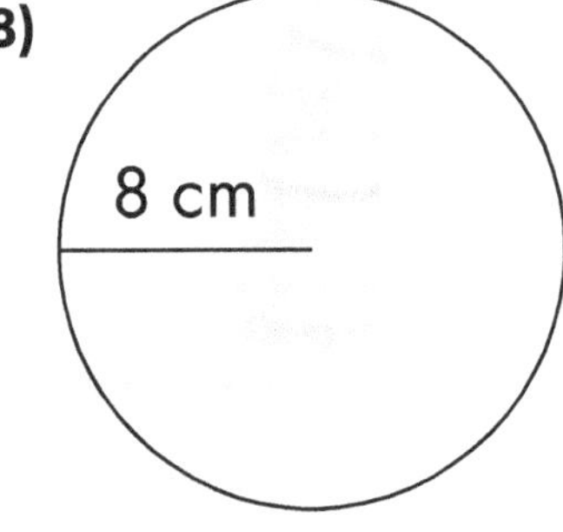

SUMMER MATH WORKBOOK
NAME:
BUILDING ACTIVITIES

9)

24 cm

____

____

10)

4 cm

____

____

11)

20 cm

____

____

12)

30 cm

____

____

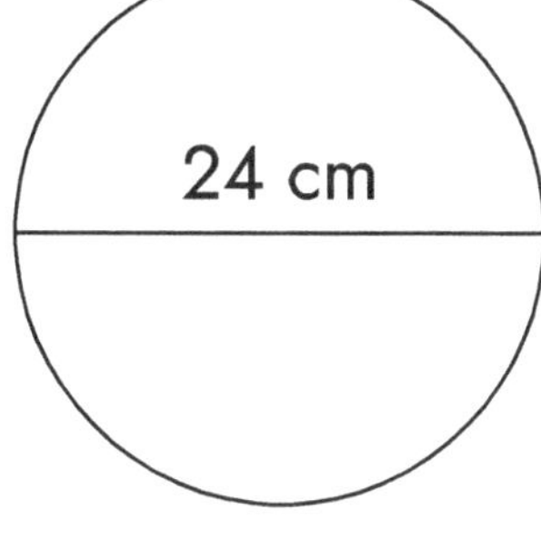

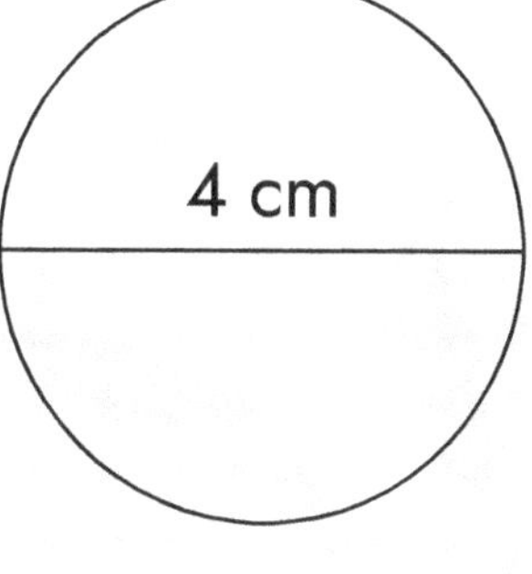

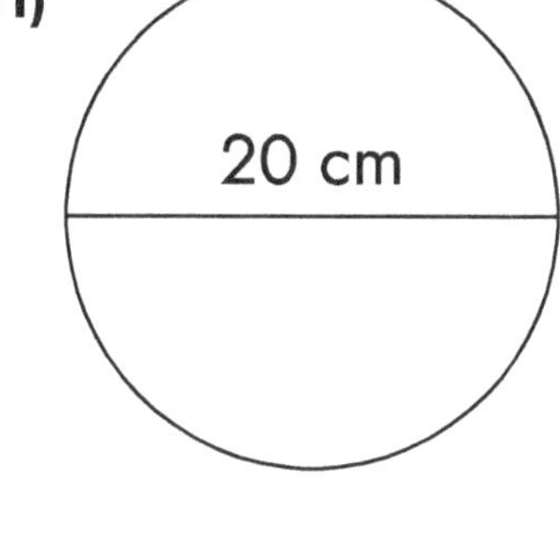

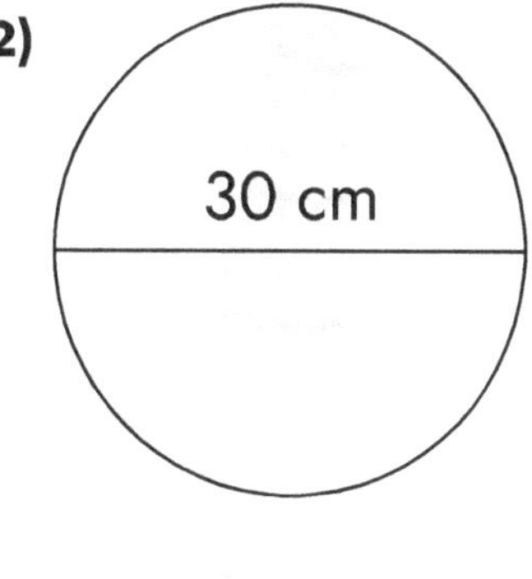

13)

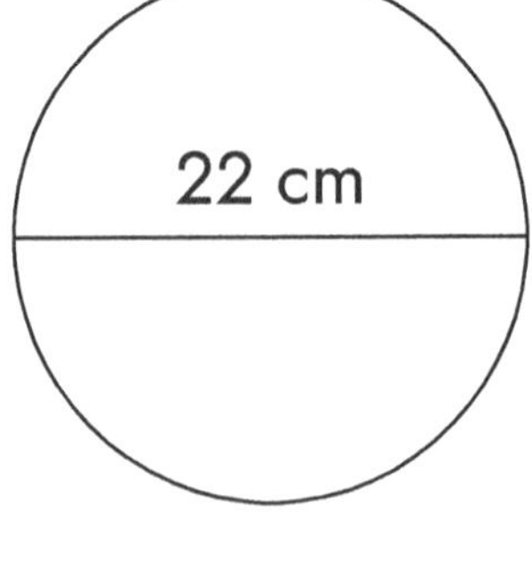

____

____

14)

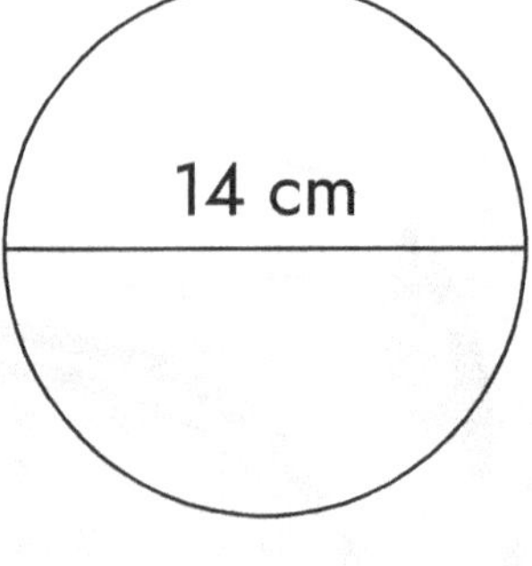

____

____

15)

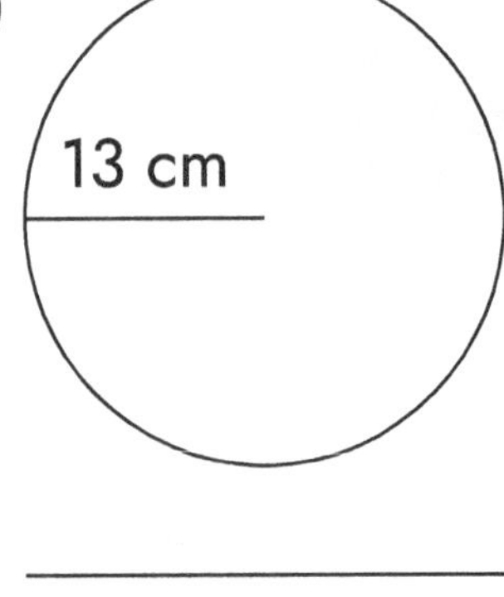

____

____

16)

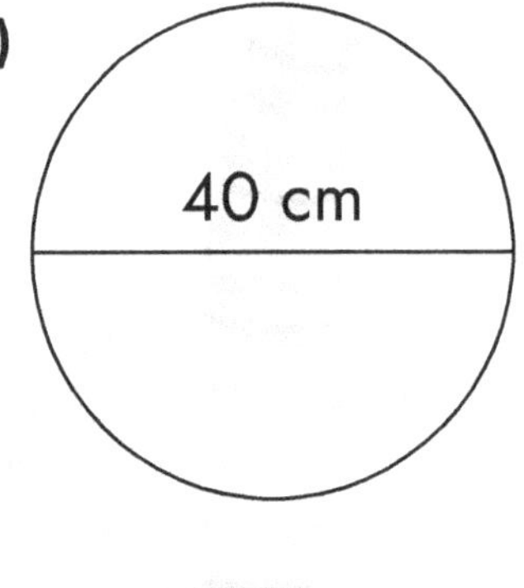

____

____

17)

19 cm

____

____

18)

18 cm

____

____

19)

1 cm

____

____

20)

17 cm

____

____

Metric Conversion

Convert the given measures.

1) 43 ft = _______________ m

2) 90 in = _______________ m

3) 40 ft = _______________ m

4) 84 in = _______________ m

5) 92 ft = _______________ m

6) 91 in = _______________ m

7) 85 ft = _______________ m

8) 33 in = _______________ m

9) 28 in = _______________ m

10) 42 ft = _______________ m

11) 46 ft = _______________ m

12) 91 ft = _______________ m

13) 34 in = _______________ m

14) 63 in = _______________ m

15) 86 in = _______________ m

16) 73 in = _______________ m

17) 48 ft = _________ m

18) 52 ft = _________ m

19) 77 in = _________ m

20) 40 ft = _________ m

21) 44 ft = _________ m

22) 11 ft = _________ m

23) 12 ft = _________ m

24) 89 ft = _________ m

25) 14 in = _________ m

26) 21 in = _________ m

27) 25 ft = _________ m

28) 47 ft = _________ m

29) 11 in = _________ m

30) 67 in = _________ m

31) 49 in = _________ m

32) 73 ft = _________ m

33) 31 ft = _________ m

34) 46 ft = _________ m

Metric Weights and Measures

Convert the given measures to new units.

1) 90 m = _________ km

2) 94 m = _________ cm

3) 73 L = _________ kL

4) 97 m = _________ cm

5) 35 m = _________ km

6) 68 t = _________ g

7) 48 kg = _________ g

8) 19 m = _________ km

9) 88 L = _________ kL

10) 27 km = _________ m

11) 32 m = _________ km

12) 71 km = _________ m

13) 42 mL = _________ kL

14) 34 kg = _________ t

15) 59 cm = _________ m

16) 95 g = _________ kg

17) 56 mL = _______________ kL

18) 80 km = _______________ m

19) 25 t = _______________ kg

20) 74 cm = _______________ km

21) 28 cm = _______________ m

22) 45 kg = _______________ g

23) 89 L = _______________ kL

24) 82 L = _______________ kL

25) 56 g = _______________ kg

26) 65 t = _______________ kg

27) 52 kL = _______________ L

28) 16 cm = _______________ km

29) 38 km = _______________ cm

30) 48 km = _______________ m

31) 37 t = _______________ kg

32) 76 mL = _______________ kL

ANSWERS

Page 1:   Multiplication: (3 x 3)

1. 149,272	**2.** 43,292	**3.** 455,344	**4.** 91,516	**5.** 327,414
6. 326,556	**7.** 124,425	**8.** 144,624	**9.** 419,520	**10.** 217,116
11. 274,995	**12.** 115,024	**13.** 50,042	**14.** 597,205	**15.** 220,820
16. 121,992	**17.** 110,166	**18.** 162,790	**19.** 437,647	**20.** 58,608
21. 109,068	**22.** 259,854	**23.** 150,880	**24.** 570,471	**25.** 78,980
26. 633,654	**27.** 701,680			

Page 4:   Multi Digit Multiplication

1. 403,380	**2.** 567,388	**3.** 615,342	**4.** 4,176,393	**5.** 1,226,712
6. 1,431,714	**7.** 3,468,374	**8.** 3,825,885	**9.** 4,893,808	**10.** 2,102,910
11. 2,208,564	**12.** 862,410	**13.** 278,069	**14.** 1,218,888	**15.** 321,950
16. 712,068	**17.** 6,271,292	**18.** 261,356	**19.** 1,107,427	**20.** 5,414,760
21. 2,622,301	**22.** 5,715,381	**23.** 8,556,012	**24.** 1,391,806	**25.** 2,938,950
26. 4,224,311	**27.** 3,232,316			

Page 7:   Long Division

1. 22,154.8	**2.** 6,359.8	**3.** 2,741.9	**4.** 10,121.8	**5.** 8,238.5
6. 10,249.1	**7.** 7,927.6	**8.** 9,482.5	**9.** 21,989.7	**10.** 11,742.6
11. 4,288.6	**12.** 8,078	**13.** 10,737.8	**14.** 3,346.4	**15.** 8,858.3
16. 9,833.6	**17.** 4,446.9	**18.** 14,220.8	**19.** 6,260.7	**20.** 3,103.3
21. 15,832.3	**22.** 13,525.3	**23.** 8,975.3	**24.** 5,425.3	**25.** 11,795.9

26. 20,206.3   **27.** 12,340.8   **28.** 2,955.2   **29.** 13,567   **30.** 7,184.2

Page 12:   Long Division: Remainders

1. 1,865 R13   **2.** 3,247 R10   **3.** 1,170 R8   **4.** 11,797 R2   **5.** 4,824 R7

6. 4,517 R7   **7.** 10,411 R0   **8.** 9,518 R1   **9.** 4,443 R5   **10.** 2,075 R12

11. 7,376 R7   **12.** 3,242 R6   **13.** 8,581 R4   **14.** 8,025 R8   **15.** 10,909 R0

16. 6,519 R7   **17.** 3,875 R6   **18.** 6,282 R6   **19.** 5,507 R11   **20.** 4,711 R9

Page 17:   Multiplying Decimals

1. 98.4015   **2.** 663.8310   **3.** 665.1388   **4.** 612.6807   **5.** 131.3963

6. 109.9012   **7.** 293.5250   **8.** 685.3034   **9.** 100.5720   **10.** 591.7046

11. 291.8352   **12.** 334.0910   **13.** 136.5210   **14.** 634.7838   **15.** 304.6285

16. 317.0079   **17.** 429.1140   **18.** 205.1976   **19.** 311.7400   **20.** 121.9056

21. 140.2297   **22.** 38.2080   **23.** 189.0280   **24.** 197.6820   **25.** 180.5225

26. 824.3235   **27.** 20.6387   **28.** 283.3560   **29.** 191.4220   **30.** 805.3173

31. 293.4392   **32.** 94.9053   **33.** 290.9860   **34.** 221.2448   **35.** 226.2185

36. 102.5661

Page 21:   Dividing Decimals

1. 67.692   **2.** 47.2   **3.** 73.846   **4.** 27.071   **5.** 12.143   **6.** 21.611

7. 46.158   **8.** 20.421   **9.** 11.412   **10.** 18.368   **11.** 30.357   **12.** 15.385

13. 47.643   **14.** 25.417   **15.** 55.563   **16.** 77.083   **17.** 35.688   **18.** 32.364

19. 65.75   **20.** 6.059   **21.** 49.643   **22.** 53.125   **23.** 76.167   **24.** 26.895

25. 21.75   **26.** 49.214   **27.** 8.923   **28.** 46.571   **29.** 19.714   **30.** 55.125

31. 15.083   **32.** 40.267   **33.** 47.545   **34.** 26   **35.** 53.083   **36.** 9.526

Page 25: The Power of 10

1. 2.7   **2.** 8,800   **3.** 0.96   **4.** 8.6   **5.** 1.1   **6.** 290

7. 0.6   **8.** 1.7   **9.** 310   **10.** 0.66   **11.** 0.93   **12.** 4,800

13. 980   **14.** 48,000   **15.** 260   **16.** 970   **17.** 320   **18.** 1.6

19. 5,100   **20.** 3,800   **21.** 740   **22.** 0.03   **23.** 670   **24.** 0.02

25. 1.8   **26.** 0.17   **27.** 0.76   **28.** 820   **29.** 0.07   **30.** 64,000

31. 68,000   **32.** 2

Page 27: Place Value

1. 9 millions   **2.** 8 hundredths   **3.** 2 hundred thousands

4. 3 tens   **5.** 1 thousand   **6.** 2 ten thousands

7. 4 tens   **8.** 9 ten thousands   **9.** 4 hundred thousands

10. 8 hundred thousands   **11.** 7 ones   **12.** 6 thousands

13. 9 hundreds   **14.** 8 millions   **15.** 8 ones

16. 2 ten thousands   **17.** 4 tenths   **18.** 5 hundreds

19. 0 ten thousands   **20.** 5 ten thousands   **21.** 6 ones

22. 7 tenths   **23.** 1 hundredth   **24.** 1 thousand

25. 5 ones   **26.** 3 ten thousands   **27.** 0 ten thousands

28. 9 ten thousands   **29.** 8 hundredths   **30.** 4 tenths

31. 5 ten thousands   **32.** 8 tens   **33.** 3 tens

34. 2 thousandths   **35.** 0 hundreds   **36.** 0 ten thousands

37. 7 thousands   **38.** 3 hundredths   **39.** 8 thousands

Page 32: Place Value and Expanded Notation

1. 65,384.334   **2.** 788,764.31   **3.** 960,446.31   **4.** 82,402,059

5. 1,893,731.2   **6.** 362,655.88   **7.** 5,485,852.3   **8.** 6,579,587.9

9. 76,943,318   **10.** 25,558.290   **11.** 6,881,878.7   **12.** 45,096.251

13. 6,155,487.2   **14.** 73,897.362   **15.** 4,586,118.3   **16.** 92,741.003

17. 99,065,151   **18.** 374,011.51   **19.** 958,539.65   **20.** 2,736,239.9

21. 82,762.634   **22.** 1,303,627.2   **23.** 1,651,280.4   **24.** 7,242,912.9

25. 38,791,766   **26.** 360,442.84   **27.** 34,954,386   **28.** 40,666,427

Page 39: Place Value and Expanded Notation

1. 9 ten thousands + 5 thousands + 7 tens + 2 ones + 2 tenths + 3 thousandths

2. 7 millions + 3 hundred thousands + 3 ten thousands + 8 hundreds + 9 tens + 6 ones

3. 8 ten thousands + 2 thousands + 8 hundreds + 6 tens + 3 ones + 5 tenths + 6 hundredths

4. 5 ten thousands + 6 thousands + 9 hundreds + 1 ten + 5 ones + 6 tenths + 3 hundredths + 9 thousandths

5. 1 ten thousand + 8 tenths + 2 hundredths + 9 thousandths

6. 1 million + 5 hundred thousands + 1 ten thousand + 4 thousands + 8 hundreds + 9 tens + 3 ones

7. 4 hundred thousands + 2 ten thousands + 3 thousands + 4 hundreds + 4 tens + 5 ones + 6 tenths

8. 7 millions + 2 hundred thousands + 4 ten thousands + 6 hundreds + 6 tens + 8 ones + 4 tenths

9. 4 ten thousands + 5 thousands + 4 hundreds + 6 tens + 1 one + 5 hundredths + 2 thousandths

10. 6 hundred thousands + 8 ten thousands + 6 tens + 1 one + 8 hundredths

11. 9 ten thousands + 8 thousands + 9 tens + 9 ones + 2 tenths + 9 hundredths + 6 thousandths

12. 1 million + 6 hundred thousands + 8 ten thousands + 3 thousands + 4 hundreds + 9 tens + 4 ones + 3 tenths

13. 8 millions + 2 hundred thousands + 9 ten thousands + 8 thousands + 4 hundreds + 1 ten + 3 ones

14. 7 ten thousands + 7 thousands + 6 hundreds + 8 tens + 4 ones + 1 tenth + 8 hundredths + 1 thousandth

15. 6 millions + 3 hundred thousands + 3 ten thousands + 5 thousands + 9 hundreds + 8 tens + 4 ones

16. 8 millions + 2 hundred thousands + 7 ten thousands + 6 thousands + 6 tens + 1 one + 6 tenths

17. 2 millions + 5 hundred thousands + 4 ten thousands + 1 thousand + 6 hundreds + 2 tens + 7 tenths

18. 7 ten millions + 1 million + 3 hundred thousands + 1 ten thousand + 9 thousands + 8 hundreds + 2 tens + 9 ones

19. 3 hundred thousands + 8 ten thousands + 4 thousands + 3 hundreds + 4 tens + 6 ones + 8 tenths

20. 8 millions + 5 hundred thousands + 6 ten thousands + 8 thousands + 9 hundreds + 7 ones + 5 tenths

21. 6 hundred thousands + 2 ten thousands + 3 thousands + 3 tens + 7 ones + 1 tenth + 3 hundredths

22. 6 ten thousands + 1 thousand + 1 hundred + 1 ten + 2 ones + 6 tenths + 5 hundredths + 3 thousandths

23. 5 ten thousands + 5 thousands + 4 hundreds + 1 ten + 7 ones + 9 tenths + 3 hundredths + 2 thousandths

24. 8 millions + 1 hundred thousand + 2 ten thousands + 9 thousands + 3 hundreds + 9 tens + 4 ones + 7 tenths

25. 5 ten millions + 2 millions + 9 hundred thousands + 4 ten thousands + 9 thousands + 5 hundreds + 8 tens + 1 one

26. 7 hundred thousands + 7 ten thousands + 4 thousands + 6 hundreds + 5 tens + 2 ones + 4 tenths

27. 6 hundred thousands + 7 ten thousands + 8 thousands + 2 hundreds + 5 tens + 5 ones + 1 tenth + 9 hundredths

28. 6 hundred thousands + 2 ten thousands + 3 thousands + 4 hundreds + 8 tens + 6 tenths + 1 hundredth

29. 7 millions + 2 hundred thousands + 3 ten thousands + 6 thousands + 3 hundreds + 6 tens + 2 ones + 7 tenths

Page 45:   Lowest Common Multiple

1. 10 **2.** 28 **3.** 12 **4.** 30 **5.** 24 **6.** 10 **7.** 6 **8.** 6 **9.** 21

10. 45 **11.** 8 **12.** 8 **13.** 24 **14.** 90 **15.** 36 **16.** 30 **17.** 63 **18.** 20

19. 8 **20.** 30 **21.** 56 **22.** 30 **23.** 70 **24.** 36 **25.** 18 **26.** 6 **27.** 35

28. 14 **29.** 9

Page 50:   Equivalent Fractions

1. 49 **2.** 117 **3.** 126 **4.** 4 **5.** 56 **6.** 114 **7.** 12 **8.** 20 **9.** 11

10. 54 **11.** 30 **12.** 1 **13.** 14 **14.** 5 **15.** 5 **16.** 60 **17.** 40 **18.** 8

19. 7 **20.** 30 **21.** 12 **22.** 1

Page 52:   Fractions Addition: Uncommon Denominator

1. 21/22 **2.** 34/45 **3.** 139/176 **4.** 81/182 **5.** 5/12

6. 37/57 **7.** 17/40 **8.** 4/5 **9.** 13/60 **10.** 13/15

11. 23/34   **12.** 11/16   **13.** 197/204   **14.** 37/42   **15.** 1/1

16. 111/140   **17.** 5/6   **18.** 23/38   **19.** 7/10   **20.** 23/30

21. 32/33   **22.** 1/2   **23.** 59/72   **24.** 83/140   **25.** 19/45

26. 9/10   **27.** 73/221   **28.** 21/34   **29.** 89/190   **30.** 35/132

31. 23/130   **32.** 11/14   **33.** 8/15   **34.** 9/20   **35.** 100/117

36. 15/28

Page 55: Fractions Subtraction: (Uncommon Denominator)

1. 3/8   **2.** 1/26   **3.** 3/55   **4.** 5/18   **5.** 53/304

6. 3/65   **7.** 1/2   **8.** 1/40   **9.** 4/153   **10.** 3/5

11. 3/34   **12.** 3/10   **13.** 1/2   **14.** 158/247   **15.** 5/22

16. 8/15   **17.** 73/170   **18.** 17/171   **19.** 15/34   **20.** 1/10

21. 5/13   **22.** 1/5   **23.** 7/30   **24.** 64/143   **25.** 13/24

26. 47/63   **27.** 1/4   **28.** 7/20   **29.** 1/57   **30.** 1/4

31. 115/171   **32.** 1/6   **33.** 19/68   **34.** 3/28   **35.** 61/112

36. 1/8   **37.** 5/12   **38.** 7/20

Page 58: Fractions Multiplication

1. 2/27   **2.** 25/44   **3.** 8/15   **4.** 5/14   **5.** 2/77   **6.** 3/8

7. 1/3   **8.** 1/10   **9.** 2/11   **10.** 3/8   **11.** 4/81   **12.** 1/3

13. 2/15   **14.** 1/36   **15.** 1/16   **16.** 4/11   **17.** 5/12   **18.** 1/20

19. 1/18   **20.** 9/14   **21.** 4/15   **22.** 1/9   **23.** 1/14   **24.** 1/7

25. 14/27   **26.** 3/5   **27.** 3/88   **28.** 3/11   **29.** 21/110   **30.** 1/5

31. 2/9   **32.** 3/8   **33.** 2/15   **34.** 1/15   **35.** 3/14   **36.** 1/12

Page 61: Fractions Division

1. 7/18   **2.** 2   **3.** 2/3   **4.** 2 11/12   **5.** 4/5   **6.** 3 2/3

7. 1/2   **8.** 1 1/5   **9.** 1/2   **10.** 27/56   **11.** 2/11   **12.** 8/15

13. 1/2   **14.** 5/6   **15.** 5 2/5   **16.** 3/7   **17.** 1 1/4   **18.** 2 2/3

19. 5   **20.** 48/55   **21.** 1/2   **22.** 12/25   **23.** 3 1/3   **24.** 33/80

25. 25/27   **26.** 1 1/2   **27.** 6/11   **28.** 1 7/18   **29.** 3/20   **30.** 2/7

31. 2   **32.** 11/18   **33.** 9/20   **34.** 1 3/7   **35.** 1 1/3   **36.** 3/4

Page 64: Area and Perimeter

1. P=40 A=96   **2.** P=19 A=16.35   **3.** P=42 A=110

4. P=38 A=90   **5.** P=24 A=36   **6.** P=30 A=43.3

7. P=34 A=49.5   **8.** P=49 A=114.45   **9.** P=26 A=28

10. P=27 A=35.07   **11.** P=26 A=27   **12.** P=22 A=22.26

13. P=19 A=15   **14.** P=27 A=35.07   **15.** P=44 A=82.5

16. P=30 A=40   **17.** P=34 A=49.5   **18.** P=55 A=127.5

19. P=26 A=42   **20.** P=45 A=84   **21.** P=46 A=130

22. P=21 A=19   **23.** P=51 A=125.14   **24.** P=33 A=52.39

25. P=19 A=16.35   **26.** P=25 A=29.02   **27.** P=42 A=84.87

28. P=25 A=29.02   **29.** P=30 A=43.3   **30.** P=27 A=32

31. P=53 A=117   **32.** P=45 A=82.5   **33.** P=24 A=24.5

34. P=27 A=32   **35.** P=34 A=50   **36.** P=37 A=60

Page 73: Area and Circumference

1. C=31.40 cm A=78.50 cm^2 **2.** C=37.68 cm A=113.04 cm^2

3. C=100.48 cm A=803.84 cm^2

4. C=25.12 cm A=50.24 cm^2

5. C=18.84 cm A=28.26 cm^2

6. C=56.52 cm A=254.34 cm^2

7. C=87.92 cm A=615.44 cm^2

8. C=50.24 cm A=200.96 cm^2

9. C=75.36 cm A=452.16 cm^2

10. C=12.56 cm A=12.56 cm^2

11. C=62.80 cm A=314.00 cm^2

12. C=94.20 cm A=706.50 cm^2

13. C=69.08 cm A=379.94 cm^2

14. C=43.96 cm A=153.86 cm^2

15. C=81.64 cm A=530.66 cm^2

16. C=125.60 cm A=1,256.00 cm^2

17. C=119.32 cm A=1,133.54 cm^2

18. C=113.04 cm A=1,017.36 cm^2

19. C=6.28 cm A=3.14 cm^2

20. C=106.76 cm A=907.46 cm^2

Page 78:   Metric Conversion

1. 13.106   **2.** 2.286   **3.** 12.192   **4.** 2.134   **5.** 28.042   **6.** 2.311

7. 25.908   **8.** 0.838   **9.** 0.711   **10.** 12.802   **11.** 14.021   **12.** 27.737

13. 0.864   **14.** 1.600   **15.** 2.184   **16.** 1.854   **17.** 14.630   **18.** 15.850

19. 1.956   **20.** 12.192   **21.** 13.411   **22.** 3.353   **23.** 3.658   **24.** 27.127

25. 0.356   **26.** 0.533   **27.** 7.620   **28.** 14.326   **29.** 0.279   **30.** 1.702

31. 1.245   **32.** 22.250   **33.** 9.449   **34.** 14.021

Page 80:   Metric Weights and Measures

1. 0.090   **2.** 9,400   **3.** 0.073   **4.** 9,700

5. 0.035   **6.** 68,000,000   **7.** 48,000   **8.** 0.019

9. 0.088   **10.** 27,000   **11.** 0.032   **12.** 71,000

13. 0.000042   **14.** 0.034   **15.** 0.59   **16.** 0.095

17. 0.000056   **18.** 80,000   **19.** 25,000   **20.** 0.00074

21. 0.28

22. 45,000

23. 0.089

24. 0.082

25. 0.056

26. 65,000

27. 52,000

28. 0.00016

29. 3,800,000

30. 48,000

31. 37,000

32. 0.000076